THE LORD'S PRAYER

Jesus Teaches Us How to Pray

Mary Lou Redding

UPPER ROOM BOOKS®
NASHVILLE

THE LORD'S PRAYER
Jesus Teaches Us How to Pray
Copyright © 2011 by Mary Lou Redding
All rights reserved.

The Upper Room® Web site http://www.upperroom.org

UPPER ROOM®, UPPER ROOM BOOKS® and design logos are trademarks owned by The Upper Room®, A Ministry of GBOD®, Nashville, Tennessee. All rights reserved.

Selection from *Gates of Prayer: The New Union Prayerbook,* ed. Chaim Stern (New York: Central Conference of American Rabbis, 1975) is used by permission. All rights reserved.

Scripture quotations are from New Revised Standard Version Bible, copyright © 1989 National Council of the Churches of Christ in the United States of America. Used by permission. All rights reserved.

Scripture quotation marked (NIV) is taken from the Holy Bible, New International Version®. NIV®. Copyright 1973, 1978, 1984 by Biblica, Inc.™ Used by permission of Zondervan. All rights reserved worldwide. www.zondervan.com

Scripture marked KJV is from the King James Version Bible.

"Clean White Boxes" by Mary Lou Redding first appeared in *alive now!* May–June 1982. Used by permission.

At the time of publication all Web sites referenced in this book were valid. However, due to the fluid nature of the Internet some addresses may have changed or the content may no longer be relevant.

Cover design: Marc Whitaker / www.mtwdesign.net
Interior design and typesetting: PerfecType, Nashville

LIBRARY OF CONGRESS CATALOGING-IN-PUBLICATION

Redding, Mary Lou
  The Lord's prayer : Jesus teaches us how to pray / Mary Lou Redding.
    p. cm.
  Includes bibliographical references (p.   ).
  ISBN 978-0-8358-1066-1
  1. Lord's prayer—Textbooks. 2. Lord's prayer—Study and teaching.. I.
Title.
  BV230.R325 2011
  226.9'60607—dc23   2011019136

Printed in the United States of America

To my co-workers at Upper Room Ministries

people whose lives and prayers are one
(most of the time)

CONTENTS

INTRODUCTION

The great church reformer Martin Luther included in his Small Catechism three essentials for every believer to know: the Ten Commandments, the Apostles' Creed, and the Lord's Prayer. Since Luther's time, leaders of the Christian church and believers on every continent have used the Ten Commandments and Jesus' model prayer as guides for daily life.

The settings of the Lord's Prayer in both places it appears in scripture—Matthew 6:9-13 and Luke 11:1-4—offer it as a prayer Jesus taught his disciples, those closest to him. As we will see during this study, those who pray this prayer from the heart are asking for a deep relationship with God, not a casual or superficial conversation. So we who want to follow Christ today can find in this model prayer a reliable guide for our praying.

THE PLAN

Each week's content has three components:
- a short chapter to read at the beginning of the week
- suggested scripture readings for five days and written responses
- a small-group meeting to end the week

You can read each week's material in about ten to fifteen minutes. The daily scripture readings (usually four or five verses) are accompanied by reflection questions and can also be completed in about ten to fifteen minutes. You will meet weekly for an hour or ninety minutes, as your group and leader decide.

JOURNALING

This book provides space where you can write responses to the reflection questions. If you want to write more than the space here allows, consider using a journal or blank book. This can be an opportunity to begin a journal if you don't already write in one. Keeping a journal is a way to deliberately pay attention to what God is doing in your life and saying to you. Note your insights from Bible reading and daily life.

If you keep a journal, you may want to bring it with you to the weekly small-group meetings. You will never be asked to reveal your responses to the reflection questions or the content of your journal, but you may want to refer to it as you discuss questions related to the week's scripture readings. Christians from every century have recommended journaling as a tool for the Christian life. I hope you will give yourself the gift of a little extra time with God through journal writing over the next six weeks.

DAILY EXAMEN

Each week you will be offered a suggestion for "daily examen" related to the section of the Lord's Prayer we're looking at that week. Daily examen is another ancient Christian practice, this one linked most closely to a particular person, Ignatius of Loyola. Ignatius taught his followers to spend time each day reflecting on how they had responded (or not) to God's call in that day's actions and attitudes. They did this by asking themselves a series of questions. We will use a simplified version of this practice.

Examen is usually done at the end of the day. The examen we will use will be one or two short questions to guide you in reflection as you lie in bed before you fall asleep. If you are like me and cannot stay awake for more than ten seconds while reclining, you may want to do your examen while sitting in a chair, before getting into bed. If you are more a morning person than a night person, you may choose to do your examen in the moments just after you awaken, before getting out of bed.

Since each week's examen builds on a familiar phrase from the Lord's Prayer, it will be easy to recall. The questions will guide you in looking back at your previous twenty-four hours. The examen is for you, not anyone else, but you may want to note in your journal or in this book any ideas or resolves that come to you during this time. These will remain private unless you choose to talk about them.

GROUP GUIDELINES

Effective small groups usually operate with a set of agreements that guide their study and interaction. Here are some common ones:

PRAYER: Group members will pray for one another and for the leader(s) between weekly sessions. (This is, after all, a group to learn about prayer.)

PRESENCE: Group members will be present each week unless pressing circumstances dictate otherwise.

PREPARATION: Group members will complete the short daily readings and daily reflections, while realizing that life happens, which means that the level of preparation may vary from week to week.

PARTICIPATION: Group members will take part in the discussion and exploration activities, but no one will be pressured to talk at any time. You and others may simply say "pass" during any discussion if you choose not to comment. On the other hand, more talkative group members will also be careful not to monopolize conversation and will pay attention to see that less talkative participants have opportunities to speak.

COURTESY: Group members will allow one another to talk without interrupting and without offering advice or correction. Side conversations are to be avoided; group members agree to respect one another's right to be heard.

CONFIDENTIALITY: What you hear in the group is not to be repeated outside the group. Everyone will get more out of the study if all members feel able to speak freely about their spiritual and personal lives, knowing that private information will not be repeated. Of course you may talk with others about what you experience in the study, but prayer requests and personal information that may emerge in conversations during weekly meetings are not to be repeated to anyone outside the group.

ADDITIONAL AGREEMENTS: Your group may decide on other guidelines for your weekly time together or on a group service project to be done at the end of the study.

As you will read in the coming pages, prayer is not about forms but about relationship. My prayer for you is that over these weeks your praying will encompass more of life as you welcome God fully into your days, using Jesus' prayer as a guide and model for living into ever-deepening conversation with God.

———

[Jesus] was praying in a certain place, and after he had finished, one of his disciples said to him, "Lord, teach us to pray, as John taught his disciples." He said to them, "When you pray, say:
Father, hallowed be your name.
    Your kingdom come.
    Give us each day our daily bread.
  And forgive us our sins,
        For we ourselves forgive everyone indebted to us.
  And do not bring us to the time of trial."
                        —Luke 11:1-4

Pray then in this way:
Our Father in heaven,
    hallowed be your name.
    Your kingdom come.
    Your will be done,
        on earth as it is in heaven.
Give us this day our daily bread.
And forgive us our debts,
as we also have forgiven our debtors.
And do not bring us to the time of trial,
    but rescue us from the evil one.
                    —Matthew 6:9-13

ONE SIZE DOES NOT FIT ALL

Our Father in heaven, hallowed be your name.

⚬⚬⚬

May the love of your name hallow every home
and every heart.

—JEWISH SABBATH PRAYER[1]

The prayer on the opposite page, the prayer we know as the Lord's Prayer, is the oldest standard prayer in the Christian faith. Its words are prayed by many thousands if not millions of believers, in many languages, many times every day, in churches and homes around the world. It is prayed in corporate worship and prayed alone by individuals. It is prayed by sports teams in locker rooms and at the end of twelve-step meetings. Calling it the most familiar prayer in the Western world is not a stretch. People have studied it carefully and widely.

As I was talking with someone about this book, he said, "There have been lots of books written about the Lord's Prayer. Why would we need another one? What will make this one different?" Those are completely legitimate questions. Many books have been written about this prayer; I've read several of them myself. This one differs from others in several ways. First, it approaches scripture differently. Rather than taking a left-brain, scholarly, or theoretical look at the scripture passages, this study will guide you in looking at scripture passages with your heart, to see how they connect to daily life and relationships. Second, the book will approach the Lord's Prayer as a model for our praying in general. Finally, you will learn several classic Christian spiritual practices (painlessly, I promise) in the course of learning about this prayer.

IN GOOD COMPANY

Because the Lord's Prayer is so familiar, we run the risk of reciting it automatically. We may say the words unaware of their transforming meaning, unaware of what we are asking God to do, rather than praying them as an honest, intimate conversation with the One who knows us deeply and loves us completely. In this six-week study we will examine the Lord's Prayer as a model for all our praying.

Why is praying so hard? Or is it? Do we make prayer harder than it has to be?

The disciple's request, "Lord, teach us to pray," reveals two facts: (1) we are in good company when we ask questions about prayer, and (2) knowing how to pray isn't automatic. If knowing how to pray wasn't easy even for those closest to Jesus, we don't have to feel bad about our struggles with prayer. This can comfort those of us who have tried and may still be trying to establish a satisfying, sustaining pattern of prayer in our lives. Yes, some people seem to learn how to pray naturally, almost by osmosis. But apparently the one who made this request of Jesus didn't feel that the disciples were in that group. Many of us feel the same. We may be embarrassed and feel inadequate or guilty about not being better pray-ers.

When I was about to become a parent, I worried about how I would respond to my child. I did not lack knowledge about taking care of a baby. I come from a huge family, and we've all been reared in close contact with many younger brothers, sisters, cousins, nieces, and nephews. I could change diapers and bounce fussy infants. But did I know how to love my child as a mother "should"? I was anxious about whether I could make the sacrifices that are part of being a parent, on both practical and philosophical levels. When I expressed my doubts, people would say things like, "The moment that baby is born, you'll feel a rush of love that will change the way you see everything," and, "Oh, don't you worry. Once that baby gets here, when it coughs or even rolls over, you'll wake up."

They were wrong about me on both of those counts. When my daughter was born, I looked down at the little stranger in my arms feeling not a rush of love but a rush of apprehension, thinking, *What have I gotten myself into?* And I did not magically become hypersensitive to sounds in the night. Our daughter could scream until the walls shook, and I wouldn't wake. My husband would wake and then cajole me toward consciousness. And I had to get to know my child and develop a bond with her just as I have to with anyone else I meet. But apparently other people took to parenting instantly. Since filling the mother role seemed to come naturally to others, I struggled with feeling that there must be something wrong with me. *Shoulds* and *oughts* are a heavy load to carry, whether we are talking about parenting or praying.

Many of us seem to believe that prayer (and other parts of the spiritual life) comes naturally to everyone else, that we're the only one who doesn't "get it." So there must be something wrong with us. But the disciples were with Jesus continually, and they still had to ask for help in learning how to pray. That should encourage us.

As Luke 11:1 tells us, the disciples asked Jesus to teach them about praying after they observed him in prayer. We can assume that they saw something in Jesus that made them want to pray as he did. Perhaps it was the power of God they saw as he healed people; perhaps it was the insight into scripture that he revealed as he taught. Whatever it was, they yearned to connect with God, to experience God's presence. And so do we all. But that doesn't mean we know how.

The disciples asked Jesus to teach them about praying after they observed him in prayer.

BEYOND RECIPES

I have asked various groups of Christians this question: How many of you feel that you pray well—as often as you should, asking for what you should, for as long as you should? In all those times, only a few people have indicated satisfaction with the way they pray. I don't think people hold back out of modesty, not wanting to brag; they hold back out of honesty. In general, people seem to feel bad about their praying.

The next phrase of Luke 11:1—"as John taught his disciples"— suggests two possible reasons. First, we have gotten the idea that we can't trust ourselves to discover—or even trust God to teach us—how to be spiritual. We turn to "experts" for instruction in how to be spiritual: "as John taught." And this questioner was going to Jesus himself, whom most Christians would call the ultimate expert.

Second, we are social creatures, and we tend to compare ourselves to others—even in our spiritual life and growth. We are tempted to assume that there is a right way to "do" every part of the spiritual life, including prayer. In prayer, as in arenas of good works, Bible study, and other religious activities, we want someone to tell us exactly what we need to do to "be good," to be spiritual in the right way.

We see evidence of this way of thinking all around us in Christian circles. People follow various recipes for the spiritual life. For prayer: the right words to say, how frequently, what to pray for, and for how long. For worship: be present every Sunday unless seriously ill; sing (or don't sing) traditional hymns; wear (or don't wear) casual clothes. For Bible reading: how often, what times of day, which passages. Some of these recipes offer charts to help people record their activity and progress: places to note prayer requests, answers to prayer and when and how they come; lists of which Bible passages to read and places to check off each reading when it's done. None of these suggestions or aids is bad, of course. For years (especially as my memory has become less reliable) I have kept a list to remind me of the people I want to bring before God when I pray. I tuck the list into the back of my current daily devotional book. But these systems can promote a limited view of what constitutes spiritual life.

Formulas for spiritual growth resemble the continual parade of diets we hear about everywhere. Creators of the latest diets make the rounds of talk shows and write books promoting diets that dictate exactly what to eat, when, and how much. Some diets specify eating only certain foods, in weird combinations—grapefruit, spinach, and hard-boiled eggs; hotdogs and bananas. Some say eat only one

Just as one-size-fits-all is a lie about clothes, it is a lie about diets— and about the spiritual life.

category of food—only fruit, only meat, only raw foods, etc. Some say eat prescribed meals every two hours. And so on. Such plans are actually efficient in some ways. For example, they take away the need to spend time making daily decisions about eating, and they certainly simplify shopping and meal preparation. The diet books sell, and these diets are popular for good reason: each of them works—for some people. But none of them works for everyone. Just as one-size-fits-all is a lie about clothes, it is a lie about diets—and about the spiritual life.

THE APPEAL OF RULES

Like us, the disciple who asked Jesus to teach him about prayer wanted to pray correctly. Living by rules can be comforting. In the spiritual life, keeping rules can make us feel that we're doing what we need to do in order to please God, that we've got it right. This desire is not new. The Gospel of Luke offers an account that makes this clear. An expert in the law comes to Jesus and asks, "What must I do to inherit eternal life?" (Luke 10:25). Jesus asks the man what the law says, and the questioner quotes from the Torah: "You shall love the Lord your God with all your heart, with all your soul, with all your strength, with all your mind; and your neighbor as yourself." These commandments focus on relationships as the essence of spiritual life.

But the lawyer wants more; he wants specifics. He asks, "And who is my neighbor?" In other words, whom do I have to love, and how much? What are the limits, the minimum I have to meet? What are the rules for this? What is the measure of whether I am doing it right? Jesus responds by telling one of the most famous parables in the Bible, the story of the good Samaritan. Even people who don't attend church often know this story: A man is beaten by robbers and left for dead. A priest passes by without helping; so does a Levite (one who works in the Temple, the equivalent of being on the staff of a church). Then a Samaritan, one of a people despised by the Jews, sees the man.

Unlike the other two, the Samaritan is moved with compassion and stops to help. He tends the man's wounds and then takes him to an inn. When the Samaritan continues his journey, he leaves money with the innkeeper to pay the expenses of caring for the injured man.

Promising to repay the innkeeper on his next trip through if he spends more, the Samaritan does not set a limit on what he will do for the injured man. The Samaritan commits himself to an open-ended relationship. This is the model of the spiritual life that Jesus commends—not rules but relationship.

I've heard people teaching about this parable say that the priest and the Levite may have passed by the injured man because they thought he was dead. Their rules for remaining ritually clean (that is, staying right with God) prohibited their touching a dead body. But the story shows that in this case keeping their rules about holiness actually led them away from the love and compassion God wants rather than toward it.

In telling this parable, Jesus indicated clearly that the spiritual life is not a predetermined course governed by a set of rules. The spiritual life is a deepening relationship with God and others. In other situations Jesus repeatedly makes this same point, refusing to be boxed in. Over and over, people ask him for rules: How many times must we forgive? Who sinned, this man or his parents, that he was born blind? In the resurrection, whose wife will she be? See Luke 6:1-10; Matthew 12:1-13, 46-50; and Matthew 15:1-20 for more examples. Each time, Jesus brings the conversations back to relationships. And so when the disciples ask Jesus to teach them to pray, it makes sense that Jesus does not begin with a description of principles and theology. In Matthew's account Jesus tells them to pray "in this way"—that is, not using these exact words but using the approach Jesus outlines. In fact, it might be useful to think of this prayer as exactly that: an outline of general categories for our praying.

WHERE PRAYER BEGINS

From the first words Jesus spoke in response, he emphasized again that prayer, like everything in the spiritual life, is about relationship. "*Our* Father" places us first of all in relationship with one another. The model that Jesus suggested does not begin with *my*. It begins with *our*.

Week 1

Opening a prayer this way is very Jewish. For Jews, prayer is a mitzvah—simultaneously a command and a privilege. Think of agents in the Secret Service who are chosen to guard the president of the United States: they shoulder the duty of protecting this leader at all costs, but being chosen for the job is an honor for them. That dual feeling and attitude can help us understand what a mitzvah is. Jews pray primarily in community. Jewish worship and prayer services require a core group of at least ten men—a minyan. Individuals may pray alone if they cannot gather with others, but that is second best. The preferred setting for prayer is in the community of believers. That assumption contrasts sharply with the go-it-alone attitude of many of us rugged individualists.

Prayer was and is deeply embedded in the Jewish faith. We usually assume that Jesus' disciples were observant Jews. Whether they were or not, Jesus certainly was, as we see in the Bible's accounts of his attending synagogue and praying regularly. But perhaps before traveling with Jesus, the disciples had been like many of us today—attending worship sporadically, praying from time to time, not really all that regular in attending to God in daily life.

Observant Jews pray regularly—at least five times a day. The Shema, drawn from Deuteronomy 6:4-9 and 11:13-21 and Numbers 15:37-41, is prayed in the morning on awakening and again before going to bed at night. Orthodox Jews pray the Shemoneh Esrei, a group of nineteen specific blessings and petitions, three times each day in synagogue. These services revolve around praying specific psalms, in a specific order—every time they gather.

In light of these Jewish prayer practices, if we step back, we probably will conclude that the one who asked Jesus for help in praying "should" have already known how to pray—coming back to those shoulds and rules. But Jesus doesn't reprimand him or scold him. This is important to notice. Jesus said that when we see him, we have seen God (John 14:8-9). When people asked Jesus for help, he did not condemn or tell them what they had done wrong. He looked at the persons before him as individuals and responded to their needs. If we believe what Jesus said, we can believe that this is how God is too—

When people asked Jesus for help, he did not condemn them.

not condemning but welcoming, no matter how much we "ought" to know about the life of prayer.

DO IT YOUR WAY

Each of us has a unique relationship with God. Think of relationship with God as you think of relationship with friends. I have one friend whom I've known since we were in elementary school. We may not talk for months, but when one of us calls the other, it's as if we spoke just yesterday. We don't have to explain why it's been so long; we don't have to apologize for the lapse. We simply enjoy the time together, and we talk deeply about what's on our hearts (as well as more superficially about what's up with the kids and our jobs and our dogs). She knows all about my weird family, and I know about hers. We don't have to explain ourselves. It is a comfortable and comforting friendship.

I have another friend whom I met only several years ago. We are in nearly daily contact. Even when one of us is traveling thousands of miles from home, we continually send text messages and e-mails. We haven't known each other nearly as long as I've known the other friend I mentioned, but the immediacy of our relationship is significant to both of us. Am I a better friend to one of these women than the other? Is one of these a better friend to me than the other? Is one friend more important than the other? No. Each of them has a unique and special place in my life, and I am richer for my ties to each of them. The relationships are simply different. Extrovert that I am, I have friendships with many other people, each one valuable and valued—and each different from all the others.

*Communicating
with God does
not rely on
magic words.*

Relationship with God is something like that variation in friendships. The way I talk to God and listen to God is unique to my relationship with God. My relationships with these friends don't depend on requirements and schedules. Communicating with God does not rely on magic words that will impress God or open the door to getting what we want. It's not a matter of checking in with God at some exact time every morning or evening. A mother does not worry about grammar, spelling, and punctuation but about receiving a letter from her child. In the same way, God isn't concerned about form but about

Week 1

connection. Prayer is a gift that forms the cornerstone of our connection with God. Or, as Abraham Joshua Heschel puts it:

> All things have a home: the bird has a nest, the fox has a hole, the bee has a hive. A soul without prayer is a soul without a home. Weary, sobbing, the soul, after roaming through a world festered with aimlessness, falsehoods, and absurdities, seeks a moment in which to gather up its scattered life, . . . in which to call for help without being a coward. . . . For the soul, home is where prayer is.[2]

The pattern for praying that Jesus gave us begins by asking us to enter a close relationship with God, inviting us to find our soul's home. But just as there are many ways to be friends, there are many ways to build a relationship with God.

NAMING GOD

One of the most remarkable insights to be drawn from the Lord's Prayer is that each of us gets to "name" God. As amazing as that sounds, in this prayer Jesus told us that we get to name the relationship we want to have with the Eternal. We can make the relationship limited or expansive, close or distant. Of course the name we choose does not change God, whose unchangeable and unchanging nature is always to love us and draw us toward wholeness. But we do "name" God by the way we think of, address, and speak of God.

If we picture God as an angry avenger, we are likely to see evidence of an angry God in the world around us. If we see God as a powerful but disinterested designer who set the universe a-ticking and then sat back to watch, we are unlikely to see much evidence of God's activity around us in everyday life. And if we see God as a close and loving parent, we are apt to feel protected and valued.

The way we think of God determines what we will see of God. We can limit what God does in and through us, and for and through those around us. This may sound impossible, but do you remember the story of Jesus returning to his hometown after he began his ministry? Jesus was unable to do miracles there because of how the people responded him; he could only heal "a few sick people." Jesus left, saying that the people who know us best can stand in the way of what God wants us to do. They refused to see him as God's prophet, and that limited what God could do for them. (See Mark 6:1-6.)

A NEW PICTURE OF GOD

"Father" would have been an unusual way for Jesus and his contemporaries to address God. It is a noticeable departure from the Jewish custom in prayer. The majority of Jewish prayers begin, "Blessed are you, Lord our God, Ruler of the universe" (or "Sovereign of the universe"). This image places God far away, exalted and powerful. In Psalms 113–118, which comprise the Hallel that is prayed in each synagogue service, God is referred to as a king, a mighty rescuer, an avenger. In fact, the book of Psalms compares God to a father only three times in its 150 psalms.[3] (To see how unusual this was, consider that the psalms call or compare God to a savior more than one hundred times, a deliverer more than fifty, a king more than forty.)

Living in relationship with God . . . draws us into relationship with one another.

Dr. David L. Lieber said, "The Book of Psalms, arguably the most beautiful collection of religious prayer poetry ever compiled, is second only to the Torah in its impact on the Jewish heart, mind, and spirit."[4] Looking at the Psalms reveals how Jesus and the disciples had heard God addressed when they went to synagogue. So for Jesus to suggest that the disciples address God as father was to suggest a far warmer, intimate, and unbreakable connection with God than typically was expressed in the prayers they knew.

What does it mean to call God father? It means that all who call on God in this way acknowledge being part of one family. We are bound to one another through our common tie to the One who has made us who and what we are. This does not mean either that we are all alike or that we will always like one another. In fact, on any given day some of us may not be all that likable. But as the archbishop of Canterbury said several years ago, "There is no way of belonging to Jesus Christ except by belonging gladly and irrevocably to that glorious rag-bag of saints and fatheads who make up the 'one holy, catholic, and apostolic' church."[5] Those who call God father claim all the others of us as brothers and sisters. When we acknowledge our tie to God in this way, we accept responsibility for relationship with the rest of the family.

As I mentioned, I come from a large family—I am one of seven siblings and have more than fifty first cousins. We have all kinds of people in that mix. With some of them I share interests such as music and sports and cooking. Some I enjoy being with; others, not so much. We are a motley crew, a hodgepodge of tall, short, fair, dark, thin, and stocky in various combinations. But we are all descendants of the same grandparents. We are family. Nothing can change that, no matter how different we are from one another.

The same is true for all of us who are Christ-followers. Living in relationship with God inevitably and irrevocably draws us into relationship with one another. Dorotheus of Gaza suggested a memorable illustration for this truth. Picture God as the center of a wheel and each of us positioned on spokes that connect us to God, to the center. As we move along the spokes of the wheel toward the Center, growing closer to God, we move closer to one another as well. Praying in harmony with what Jesus did and taught always moves us toward others.

GOD'S NATURE OR GOD'S NAME?

Talking about the opening of this prayer leads us naturally into considering how we address God. In offering this model for prayer, Jesus was not telling us God's name. Jews revere God's name deeply and believe human lips are unworthy even to utter the name of the Holy One. In fact, Jewish writers, teachers, and rabbis refer to "the Name" rather than ever pronouncing God's name itself. This is why in Hebrew Scripture (Old Testament) the word *lord* when used to translate God's name is represented in English by four capital letters, the last three smaller than the first, like this: LORD. (Lord with lowercase o-r-d indicates that a different word has been translated from the Hebrew.)

Those four letters in that presentation indicate that they are a substitution for the four Hebrew letters Y-H-W-H, the consonants of God's name. Jews usually substitute the word *Adonai*, which means Lord, in places where Y-H-W-H appears. Scribes indicate to readers of the Torah to say Adonai rather than pronounce God's name by adding the vowel points for the word Adonai to the four letters Y-H-W-H.[6] Jews so reverence God's name and the word *God* that a Web site about Judaism tells users if they print from the Web site any content that includes the word *God,* they should handle the paper carefully as a sign of respect for God's name.[7]

From this information about how Jews regard God's name, we know that Jesus was not saying that God's name is "Father." As a devout Jewish person, Jesus would not have said the name of God. Jesus was instead telling us something about God's nature: God desires close relationship with us and welcomes us as beloved children would be welcomed by a loving parent.

A NEW NAME

For some of us (I am one of them), the image of God as a father is difficult and limiting. If we grew up with a distant, absent, critical, abusive, or otherwise ineffective father, calling God father may connect our image of God to painful memories and disturbing feelings. For me, calling God father does not open the door to a welcoming relationship. My images of self-sacrificing love and constancy come from observing my mother. So if Jesus were teaching me to pray and trying to help me understand the relationship God wants to have with me, he might suggest that I call God mother.

What we call God is important; it is anchored to our emotions, even though we may be unaware of that. The fact that some people become upset at hearing God addressed in unfamiliar ways demonstrates the emotional ties to names for God. While calling God father reveals something of the relationship God wants with us, others might understand that relationship better by calling God mother. The issue is not the word we use for God but what image of God enables us to know God's love, approach God gladly, and feel that we are warmly welcomed.

Some people grew up in churches or traditions that named or described God more often as a judge than as a loving parent. Bible verses such as "Serve the LORD with fear, with trembling kiss his feet, or he will be angry and you will perish in the way; for his wrath is quickly kindled" (Ps. 2:11) evoke uncomfortable emotional memories. God has been painted too often as an avenger surrounded by eternal fire. Jesus' model prayer invites us to look at God differently, to discover that no matter what we have experienced—the best and the worst—the relationship God offers is far richer, deeper, and more healing than we have ever had with any person. Whatever we need to call God in order to enter fully into that relationship, Jesus would no doubt approve of.

THAT FAR-OFF GOD

The next phrase of the prayer—"in heaven, hallowed be your name"—reminds us of an amazing truth: the Holy One has built a bridge to us. This God who wants to be as close to us as a beloved relative is also the "Sovereign of the universe," the Creator of all that is. Yet this God chooses to be in relationship with us, as impossible as that seems. Jesus is the proof that God will do whatever it takes to reach us. (See John 1:1-18 and Phil. 2:1-11.) God actually became a human being in order to prove to us that we are loved and sought out. Even so, Jesus as an observant Jew goes on to remind us that whatever name we use when we speak to God, we are meant to "hallow" that name.

The essence of prayer is . . . allowing ourselves to be known by God.

The word *hallowed* sounds strange to our modern ears. About the only word most of us can compare it to is *Halloween*—a contraction of All Hallows' Eve, the eve of All Saints' Day. All Saints' Day, November 1, is the day in the Christian calendar when we honor all the holy people who have "died in the faith." *To hallow* means "to make holy." How could we ever do that—make God holy—when we are human and sinful? A Jewish sabbath prayer offers a way to think about that. The prayer says:

> You are holy, Your name is holy, and those who strive to be holy declare Your glory day by day. Blessed is the Lord, the holy God.[8]

When we try to live as God wants us to, we show that we honor who God is—Absolute Holiness. Our actions say to the world that we honor God, and all that people see of God's holy nature they will see in us or not at all.

One paradox of prayer as Jesus taught it is this: we who are far from holy are lovingly invited and welcomed to come close to God who is holy beyond our imagining. By honoring this relationship, we simultaneously acknowledge both the holiness and the mercy of God.

The essence of prayer is being with God as we are, opening ourselves to the amazing possibilities that come with knowing God, and allowing ourselves to be known by God. Each time we approach God in the spirit that Jesus suggested, we signal again that we are accepting God's invitation to relationship. We are committing ourselves to God and to all the others who pray along with us.

WEEK 1 DAILY EXAMEN

Each day this week, either before you get out of bed in the morning or before you fall asleep at night, look back over the preceding twenty-four hours. Then think about this question:

How did I welcome God and honor God's holiness?

DAILY SCRIPTURE READING AND REFLECTION

Day 1: Read Psalm 27:1-3, 9-10.

1 How is God like light? What does light do for us physically that God does for us spiritually? How would your life today have been different if you had no electricity?

2 In what sense is God a "stronghold"? How has God been a hideout for you?

3 What trait of God makes you less fearful of what life may bring? How has your sense of that trait made a difference to you in a daily situation?

Day 2: Read Romans 8:14-17.

1 What do you call God most often when you pray? Why do you use this name for God? What about this image of God draws you toward God?

2 What about your father provides a picture of God that appeals to you? What about your father provides an image of God that could block an open relationship with God?

3 What does the "Spirit bearing witness with our spirit" refer to? If emotion, what limit do emotions have as a gauge of spiritual life? If something else, what is it and how does this witness become apparent to us?

Day 3: Read Psalm 23.

1 If you were creating a movie to convey the emotion and the truth in this psalm, what would the setting be? What kind of music would you use for the sound track? Why would you make these choices?

2 Which verse of this psalm elicits the strongest response from you? Why? Which verse do you forget? Why is this verse forgettable for you?

3 What does a shepherd do for sheep that God does for you physically and spiritually?

Day 4: Read Psalm 118:1-5.

1 Sit quietly for a few minutes and consider the phrase "steadfast love." What memories, images, or thoughts rise within you as you ponder it?

2 If you were writing a praise litany like the one in these verses, what trait or action of God would you mention instead of "steadfast love"? What groups or individuals would you invite to join you in this praise?

3 Who has been for you an image of steadfast love? How do such examples help you to understand God's love?

Day 5: Read Deuteronomy 6:4-6.

1 Suppose someone asked your family or close friends whether you experience and express your relationship with God more with your heart (your emotions), your soul (your instincts and natural inclinations), or your might (your actions). How would the people who know you well be likely to answer, and why?

2 What can we do to "keep . . . in [our] heart[s]" what we believe is true about God?

3 Observant Jews mount these verses (and others) inside a small cylinder (a mezuzah) on the door frame of their home. Each time they leave, they touch the cylinder as a sign of their love for God. Would you consider adopting this practice? Why or why not? How might doing this affect our behavior, if at all?

PREPARING FOR THE GROUP MEETING

If you have time, look back over your daily reflection pages and journal, and make some notes in response to these questions:

If you did the daily examen, what is your response to the practice? How did it change you or your actions?

Which of the week's scripture passages related to a personal concern?

What in this week's readings most challenged or surprised you?

MEETING NOTES/RESPONSES

WHO'S IN CHARGE HERE?

Your kingdom come, your will be done, on earth as it is in heaven.

———

I am the master of my fate:
I am the captain of my soul.

—FROM "INVICTUS" BY WILLIAM ERNEST HENLEY

People in the United States don't know much about what it feels like to have a king or queen. Those of us who grew up in the U.S. have never lived under a monarch, and most of us can probably name only a few of the seven ranks of royalty. (We pause here for those who are of the persuasion to have to try to name all seven of them.) When we refer to God as a king or use the word *lord*, we do not intend a political meaning and don't even really think about what the word means. *Lord* is primarily a name for God. In fact, if we were asked what the next rank below a lord or lady is or what the opposite of a peer, or lord, is, most of us wouldn't know. (It's a commoner. That distinction is reflected in the House of *Lords*—"Peers"—and the House of *Commons* in the British Parliament.)

So when we talk about God having a kingdom or being a king, it's a concept we know little of and have no firsthand emotional response to. And when we pray, "your kingdom come, your will be done, on earth as it is in heaven," we don't realize what we're asking, what radical change we are inviting God to make.

Not so for Jesus' hearers. The people of Israel had been subject to many monarchs. In Samuel's time they begged for a king so they could be like other nations. Their most famous king, David, is an ancestor of Jesus. Kings as they knew them were absolute rulers. They demanded taxes, and people could be put to death for disobedience to them. Kings could be pretty scary characters. Samuel told the people of Israel what would happen if they had a king:

> [A king] will take your sons and appoint them to his chariots and to be his horsemen, and to run before his chariots; and he will appoint for himself commanders of thousands and commanders of fifties, and some to plow his ground and to reap his harvest, and to make his implements of war and the equipment of his chariots. He will take your daughters to be perfumers and cooks and bakers. He will take the best of your fields and vineyards and . . . one-tenth of your grain. . . . and your male and female slaves, and the best of your cattle and donkeys. . . . and you shall be his slaves.—1 Samuel 8:11-17

Samuel was right in saying all this, of course. The people of Israel had come to know about absolute rulers.

WHO WANTS A KING?

The everyday Jewish prayers of praise familiar to Jesus' hearers begin, "Blessed is the Lord our God, Ruler of the universe," or, "Sovereign of the universe." Each time they pray, observant Jews name God as the one who is in charge. Contrast that with our individualistic attitudes: "A man's home is his castle"; "I am the master of my fate"; "Look out for number one"; "What I do is no one's business but my own." We will be subject to no one. That is a foregone conclusion in the U.S. We don't even want a federal government that legislates behaviors—at least not behaviors that we don't agree with.

However, praying for God's kingdom to be established here on earth presupposes that there will a king—and it will not be us. When we pray for God's kingdom to come, we are saying that we will no longer be in charge, that God will be directing what happens. Though I have no idea what having a king and being subject to one actually feels like, my first response is to think that no matter how benevolent any king might be, I would still prefer to call the shots myself, to set my own agenda and plan my own course. But this way of praying says that we are giving up that mind-set. These fourteen words invite God to turn our world and its usual way of doing things on its ear. We are asking for the reign of God within human hearts and over the world as a whole.

One of my friends attends a church where members pray a version of the Lord's Prayer different than the usual translation. They pray, "Our Father and Mother . . . thy kin-dom come . . . ," in order to use language that includes everyone. *Kin-dom* is not an actual English word, but it is no more artificial, really, than our calling God a king. We don't have referents for king and kingdom in our experience either. Asking for God's kin-dom to come fits with beginning the prayer by saying "Our Father": it places us in community, among "kin," as a family. The really troublesome and meddlesome words are the next ones: "Your will be done, on earth as it is in heaven."

In God's domain, when God is in charge, God's vision for the world prevails. I love the passage in the *Messiah* that goes, "The kingdom of this world is become the kingdom of our Lord, and of his Christ, and of his Christ; And He shall reign for ever and ever." Those lines build on Revelation 11:15 in the King James Version of the Bible. When we ask for God's will to be done on earth as it is in heaven, we are praying for the entire cosmos to bend toward what God wants.

We are praying for an end to hunger, an end to war, an end to greed (and its reverse side, poverty), to lying, to all forms of cruelty and exploitation—to all that harms people and blocks the fullness of life that Jesus came to bring us. (See John 10:10.) We are praying for a different kind of world. This part of Jesus' outline for prayer leads us naturally into intercession, into praying for those who are not experiencing the life God wants for us all. When we see people in need, we know that God's will is to meet their needs, and so we pray for God's will to be done in their circumstances.

OPENING THE DOOR

When we ask for God's ways to prevail in the world, in effect we are also praying to be changed ourselves. As my former pastor once said, "God's kingdom cannot come until our kingdom goes."[1]

God's kingdom is described in several ways in the Gospel of Matthew, the Gospel that talks most about it. A series of parables in chapter 13 compares God's kingdom to sowing seed, to a mustard seed/bush, to yeast, to a treasure, to fine pearls, and to a net. Two of these parables describe people who sell all that they have in order to acquire the treasure that is the kingdom of God (Matt. 13:44-46). "All" does not mean just a sizable portion of; all is everything, holding nothing back.

Living in God's kingdom, as God wants us to live, means giving God access to every part of our lives. "All" means we welcome God into our job; our finances; our choices about how we spend our time; our relationships with family, friends, and enemies; our politics; how we care for our bodies; the way we treat clerks in stores; how we drive—all of it. I don't know about you, but I block God out in some of those places. Praying for God's kingdom to come means that I am opening the door to God in all those areas I named and all the other ones I'm not even aware of yet. Saying that I want to pursue life in God's realm means that I cannot continue to live my life for myself, by myself, as I choose.

We try to make God's will something obscure in order to duck out of doing something or, sometimes, anything.

RECOGNIZING GOD'S WILL—OR NOT

One of the ways we weasel out of living what we pray for in the Lord's Prayer is saying that we don't know what God's will is. This is often a cop-out or a stalling tactic. In many places the Bible is stunningly clear about what God wants. Quoting my former pastor Howard Olds again: "It is the will of God that the naked be clothed, the sick cared for, the hungry fed. What part of this do you not understand?"[2] Those words remind me of a quote attributed to Mark Twain: "It ain't those parts of the Bible that I can't understand that bother me, it is the parts that I do understand." We try to make God's will something obscure in order to duck out of doing something or, sometimes, anything. The Bible offers many unequivocal directives about what God wants:

Welcome everyone into your church. (Jas. 2:1-5, 9)

Visit the sick and those in prison. (Matt. 25:36)

Be honest in business dealings. (Mark 10:19; 1 Thess. 4:6)

Don't go to bed angry. (Eph. 4:26)

Enjoy what God has given you. (1 Tim. 6:17)

Treat rich and poor with the same respect. (Jas. 2:9)

Speak the truth in love. (Eph. 4:15, 25, 29)

Don't exploit one another. (1 Thess. 4:6)

Do good to those who hate you. (Luke 6:27)

Forgive one another. (Col. 3:13)

Make peace with those who anger you. (Matt. 5:22-24; Rom. 12:18)

Give generously and lend to those who ask. (Luke 6:30, 35; 2 Cor. 9:6-9)

Pray for governmental leaders. (1 Tim. 2:1-2)

Be an example in your speech, your love, your purity. (Matt. 5:34; 1 Tim. 4:12)

The list could go on and on. In many situations we know what God wants us to do. Pretending that we don't is a way of saying, "Let God be someone else's king but not mine—at least not right now."

The King James translation of the Bible renders this part of the Lord's Prayer, "Thy will be done in earth." More modern translations read "on earth," but the preposition *in* reminds me that we are made of earth. When we pray for God's reign to come fully, we are inviting God into the earth that is us. We are inviting God into the matter and matters of real life, right where we are. We are asking, "Do your will through me."

The other side of this petition offers a welcome truth: we don't need to have all the answers. When we pray, "Your will be done," that's exactly what we're saying. We are human and limited, which means the dilemmas and challenges we face can block our view of what God wants. We are also fallible and sometimes stubborn and closed minded. These characteristics can keep us from seeing what

God wants—even though what God wants may seem clear to others. We know God's will is always directed toward our good. So when we are puzzled beyond our limits, this part of the prayer expresses our trust that God is at work in what will unfold. When we find ourselves locked in disagreement with another person or an institution, praying for God's will to be done reminds us that, as sure as we may be of our position, there is much that we do not know.

CHANGE IS A-COMIN'

When God strides into town (often looking remarkably like you and me and the other folks who are praying this prayer), we know that change is afoot. If the world is not what God wants it to be, change has to come.

Tearing down must sometimes be done before building can proceed. We don't often hear the statement Simeon made about Jesus. When the young child Jesus is brought to the Temple, the faithful and expectant Simeon declares to Mary and Joseph, "This child is destined for the falling and the rising of many in Israel, and to be a sign that will be opposed . . . and a sword will pierce your own soul too" (Luke 2:34-35).

A disconcerting truth about transformation of people and the world is the degree of upheaval that change almost always requires. Even God-directed change looks at times like chaos. If we like our world to be neat and tidy, praying for God's kingdom to come is not the way to keep it so. Ecclesiastes tells us there is "a time to plant, and a time to pluck up what is planted; . . . a time to break down, and a time to build up; . . . a time to throw away stones, and a time to gather stones together" (Eccles. 3:2,3,5). If we don't want to rock the boat, we should avoid praying for God's will to be done. If we ask God what we can do, by one means or another, God will tell us—and the change will begin.

When we live by the values of God's kingdom, we will be changed inwardly. Our priorities will change. The criteria by which we make decisions will change. And we will be changed outwardly. The way we spend our time and energy will change.

Tearing down must sometimes be done before building can proceed.

So are you sure you want to pray for God's kingdom to come, God's will to be done? That's a dangerous prayer.

THE NEED FOR COURAGE

Recently I heard a sermon titled "Dangerous Hope." The preacher's text was Hebrews 11—all forty verses. This passage of scripture includes a lengthy list of those who lived "by faith" because they believed in and worked for what God asked them to do: "By faith Moses was hidden by his parents for three months after his birth, . . . and they were not afraid of the king's edict" (there's an illustration of what it's like to live under a king's power). Listing the acts of the faithful continues:

> By faith the people passed through the Red Sea . . . . By faith the walls of Jericho fell. . . . And what more should I say? For time would fail me to tell of Gideon, Barak, Samson, Jephthah, of David and Samuel and the prophets—who through faith conquered kingdoms, administered justice, obtained promises, shut the mouths of lions, quenched raging fire, escaped the edge of the sword, won strength out of weakness. . . .

but (here comes the dangerous part of hope)

> Others were tortured. . . . Others suffered mocking and flogging, and even chains and imprisonment. They were stoned to death, they were sawn in two, they were killed by the sword; they went about in skins of sheep and goats, destitute, persecuted, tormented—of whom the world was not worthy. They wandered in deserts and mountains, and in caves and holes in the ground.
>
> Yet all these, though they were commended for their faith, did not receive what was promised.—Hebrews 11:23, 29-30, 32-39

Doing what God asks of us takes courage, because working to make the world more like what God desires can be a thankless task, even a dangerous one. Some theologies claim that God wants us always to win and be prosperous, but scripture's witness indicates otherwise: the good guys and gals don't always win. When we pray for

Week 2

God's kingdom to come and commit ourselves to work for it, we are tying ourselves to a dangerous hope—the hope for a different kind of world, with different rules. We may see wonderful results—seas parting and walls falling—or we may work in hope without seeing much happen. But results are not the measure of faithfulness.

WHERE TO BEGIN

How do we move from praying the words "your will be done" to living them? We don't begin by trying to be Jesus. I heard a preacher say, "The question is not *How could I ever live like Jesus did?* We can't." Jesus lived in another country and a different culture, over two thousand years ago, in an agrarian society where most people were illiterate. We don't live in that world, and so our situations and calls from God are not the same. That preacher went on to suggest that the more helpful and more answerable question might be *How would Jesus live my life if he knew what I know about my surroundings, the people, and the problems?*[3]

Jesus is our definitive word about who God is (see John 14:8-9) and who we are meant to be: agents of God's healing work and whole persons ourselves. Of course, fostering the wholeness of others while attending to our own spiritual well-being is a continuing challenge. The many tasks connected with bringing wholeness to others can crowd out the prayer, meditation, and rest we need to nourish our own spirit and body. Jesus provides our model in this too. He drew aside for prayer even when crowds of needy people followed him.

Jesus said that those who believe in him would do even greater works than he did (John 14:12), but life often gets in the way of what God wants. The Gospel of Mark shows that Jesus, like us, faced constant interruptions and various pressures: while he was teaching in the synagogue, a man with an unclean spirit interrupted him (Mark 1:21-28); while he was praying, the disciples interrupted him (1:35-39); while in Capernaum, he was interrupted by a man being lowered through the roof into the room where he was teaching (2:1-4); while walking through a grainfield, he was interrupted by Pharisees (2:23-28); a crowd interrupted his eating, and his family tried to stop him as he spoke to that crowd (3:21-22); his family interrupted again as he spoke to a group of scribes (3:22-23, 31-32). This pattern continues throughout Mark's Gospel.

What we see in Jesus' responses shows us that doing the will of God is not about mapping out a path to a goal, managing our time, and developing more efficient habits so we can accomplish more. Doing the will of God is about paying attention to the people and needs around us. Jesus shows us that doing God's will focuses on noticing people, not avoiding them as interruptions.

GOING TO AFRICA

When I was a teenager, I heard a sermon about opening ourselves completely, in every area of our life, to God. The preacher focused on our being willing to dedicate all our energies and skills to God, down to and including our daily work. I wanted to do that. I remember the exact date that I offered God my future. And I began planning what would be necessary to become a missionary and prepare to spend my life in Africa. I know that my assumption is a cliché, but I truly assumed that was what I had agreed to do.

As the years unfolded, I went to a Christian college and learned more about discernment and about concentrating on serving God in each day as it arrived. In the course of that learning and with wise counsel from other believers, I discovered that for me answering God's call did not mean becoming a missionary. My talents and passions made it clear that my calling lay somewhere else. To be honest, I was a bit disappointed; I had thought living in Africa would be pretty cool. But by concentrating on listening to God one day at a time, I eventually found the place where my "deep gladness" meets the "world's deep hunger" (Frederick Buechner's idea and words). My deepest happiness comes from studying the Bible and helping people apply its truth to daily life. When I am doing what God made me to do, I experience deep joy. And I believe that is the case for each of us. When God calls us to a task, doing it energizes us and brings us satisfaction that we find nowhere else—even when the task is demanding, tiring, even risky.

Doing God's will begins with whatever we find at the end of our arms.

Week 2

Week 2

Doing God's will is not some faraway thing. Doing God's will begins with whatever we find at the end of our arms. What needs can we see and touch from where we sit right now? That's where we begin. That's our first assignment in making the world more like God wants it to be. The times that we choose to live our prayer, God's kingdom can be more clearly seen "on earth as it is in heaven."

Human nature being what it is, each day we have to choose anew whether we will allow God's will to be done in the earth that is us.

WEEK 2 DAILY EXAMEN

Each day this week, either before you get out of bed in the morning or before you fall asleep at night, look back over the preceding twenty-four hours. Then think about this question:

Where did I see a need and find joy in responding to it?

DAILY SCRIPTURE READING AND REFLECTION

Day 1: Read Micah 4:1-4.

1 What picture of God's will for you individually and for your family do you see in these verses? What picture of God's will for the wider world do you see in this passage?

2 Which part of this vision are you most drawn to, and why? Reflecting on what you've seen and heard lately, which part of this vision seems least likely to come true, and why?

3 What do you see as your part in bringing about the kind of world Micah describes? What role might your local church play in this vision? What is the role of the larger church—your denomination or all Christians?

Week 2

Day 2: Read Revelation 21:1-5; 22:1-2.

1 How do these verses affect you? If you were to set them to music, what style would the music be? Why do you make that choice?

2 Which aspects of a "new heaven and a new earth" do you most yearn to experience in your life right now? What would you like God to "make new" for you?

3 Thinking about recent news, what nations and wounds need healing? Where and how are people offering the healing touch of God in these situations? How/where is God nudging you to do something?

Day 3: Read Romans 12:1-2, 9-21.

1 What can help us to "discern what is the will of God" in specific situations? What helps you to discover God's will for you?

2 Read again verses 12-17. Which of the behaviors listed do you often struggle to show? Which have you struggled with most recently?

3 Think about your community of faith. Which individuals exemplify one or more of the attitudes and traits mentioned in this scripture passage? How do such people help us to understand and live God's will?

Week 2

Day 4: Read John 14:8-12.

1 Read verse 9 again. Jesus was a Galilean Jew and a carpenter, and of course he was not saying God is a Jewish carpenter. What do we need to filter out of our images of Jesus the Mediterranean, Jewish carpenter in order to see what Jesus shows us about God? What traits of God did Jesus embody? How is God more than what Jesus showed us?

2 Which of Jesus' traits and actions are you are glad to know characterize God? Which traits and actions of Jesus show you surprising aspects of God? Are any of these the same ones?

3 What do you think verse 12 means? Are believers and the church doing "even greater works" than Jesus did? Which works of Jesus are we meant to continue? Which works that Jesus did would you like to be part of?

Day 5: Read John 10:1-10.

1 Who do you know who lives life "to the full" (NIV) or "abundantly" (NRSV)? What actions and attitudes make you say this? Does the abundant life you see in these people have anything to do with wealth?

2 How does this passage identify for you what God's will is not? Where today did you notice God's will being blocked?

3 By what means does God speak to you or guide you? How have you come to trust that what you "hear" through this/these means is God's "voice"?

Week 2

Preparing for the Group Meeting

If you have time, look back over your daily reflection pages and journal, and make some notes in response to these questions:

If you did the daily examen, what is your response to the practice? How did it change you or your actions?

Which of the week's scripture passages related to a personal concern?

What in this week's readings most challenged or surprised you?

Meeting Notes/Responses

LIFE IS JUST SO DAILY!

Give us this day our daily bread.

—◦◦◦—

Listen. Pay attention. There is something sacred in this moment,
and it is calling your name.

—KARLA M. KINCANNON[1]

My mother-in-law was a true Southern lady. She attended Winthrop College, a small women's college at the time, in South Carolina. Winthrop taught their "young ladies" the proper way to sit and to pour tea and marched them to church on Sunday mornings in white gloves and hats. But my mother-in-law probably would have done exactly what they taught without that training. She was one of the most naturally genteel and gracious people I have ever known, and I loved her.

One tenet of Southern graciousness is to focus always on the other, the guest. My mother-in-law would never dream of doing anything to make another person uncomfortable—down to refusing to state her own wishes and preferences if she thought it might inconvenience another. For example, once when she was visiting us, as I prepared to shop for groceries I mentioned that peanut butter was on my list. I asked if she had a preference for smooth or crunchy. "Oh, either is fine with me. Just get whatever ya'll want."

"Okay. I'll get crunchy, since I got smooth last time." Having myself been brought up as a Southern female (and even though not as much a lady as she), I had been taught to read people's expressions and body language in order to try to meet their needs even if these were unexpressed. Something in her manner caught my attention. So I said, "What is it? Would you prefer smooth?"

"Well, yes, actually I would." Many of us—and perhaps this is more true in the South than other places—have been trained to defer to others even in inconsequential matters such as a choice between smooth and crunchy peanut butter. We are taught to hold back from anything that might seem to promote self. For example, we were taught in English classes the silly convention of never beginning sentences with "I," because, presumably, anyone reading what we've written wouldn't know that another person is behind the words, and we wouldn't want to give away that secret.

ASKING US TO ASK

In this week's phrase from the Lord's Prayer, Jesus tells us to bring our personal requests to God, to ask for our daily needs to be met. Yet many of us find it hard to talk to God about the stuff of every day. A clergy friend says we should not bother God with requests about the piddly details of our lives. God is concerned with the big issues, the global scale. God gave us a brain and two hands, and we're to use those in the small matters and thus free God to deal with what is truly important—and that's not us and our daily activities.

That view of prayer stands at odds with the Jewish tradition Jesus knew. Orthodox Jews pray specifically about details of their everyday life. For instance, there's a prayer to say upon waking in the morning. Jewish men say prayers related to inspecting their prayer shawl, putting it on, and wrapping it around the body. They pray specific words before placing the phylacteries (*tefillin*) around the head, another prayer before placing them around the arm, and another after wrapping the straps around the middle finger. (These phylacteries hold two vials that contain small scrolls with quotations from the Torah. These remind the wearer to love and to keep God's law. We might compare them to the rosaries Roman Catholics use to guide them through a series of specific prayers.)

THE SMALL STUFF

Orthodox Jewish daily rituals specify different prayers to be recited with various daily activities, including before and after eating, while washing the hands and before eating bread, before eating grain products, before eating fruit, before eating non-fruit produce, and before eating other foods, as well as before drinking wine. Putting on a new article of clothing calls for a certain prayer, as does a good event or a bad event or encountering something new.

Jewish religious observances in daily life extend beyond prayers. As mentioned earlier, Jewish people mount a mezuzah on the door frames of their homes. On the scroll inside is the Shema, the text of Deuteronomy 6:4-9 and 11:13-21 and Numbers 15:37-41. Those entering and leaving the home touch the mezuzah as a reminder to live the Torah's command:

> Hear, O Israel: The LORD is our God, the LORD alone. You shall love the LORD your God with all your heart, and with all your soul, and with all your might. Keep these words that I am commanding you today in your heart. Recite them to your children and talk about them when you are at home and when you are away, when you lie down and when you rise. Bind them as a sign on your hand, fix them as an emblem on your forehead, and write them on the doorposts of your house and on your gates.

The last sentence of that quotation explains the purpose of both phylacteries and the mezuzah.

For Jesus' hearers (and for us) the small acts of every day were and can be opportunities to turn our minds to God. Daily activities can become reminders to give thanks, to ask for help, and to open ourselves to God's presence as we go through our tasks. We can "hallow" these daily moments—honor the "something sacred" in each of them—by welcoming God continually.

Week 3

HONEST WITH GOD

"Give us this day our daily bread" reminds us to be honest and direct with God, to name what we need. In Matthew 20:29-34 and Mark 10:46-52 we see Jesus inviting people to do this. Jesus says to blind men in both stories, "What do you want me to do for you?" Most of us would assume what they wanted from Jesus would be self-evident. They were blind, so obviously they would want Jesus to address that. But just as we need to name the relationship we want to have with God, these men were asked to tell Jesus what they wanted and needed.

The importance of being honest with God has been known since Old Testament times. In many psalms we hear people talking openly to God about their feelings and about what they want God to do: "My God, why have you forsaken me?"(Ps. 22:1). "I am lonely and afflicted. Relieve the troubles of my heart" (Ps. 25:16-17). "O God, you have rejected us, broken our defenses; you have been angry; now restore us!" (Ps. 60:1). Open the Bible to almost any page in the book of Psalms to find similar honest cries. In this part of his prayer "outline," Jesus encourages us to bring our needs to God as part of our praying, every day.

Jesus' advice to ask God for what we need confirms that God cares about the practical side of life and about us as individuals. Matthew 10:30 declares God knows the number of hairs on our head—so God must update our status every time we wash or brush our hair. We realize that God is closely involved with us, and we are meant to make our ordinary, physical needs a matter of prayer. God wants us to ask. We make these requests not because God is unaware of our needs; we ask as a way to acknowledge our dependence on and trust in God.

I try not to pry into my adult daughter's life, so I don't usually ask her questions beyond something like, "How's your week going?" or, "Got any big plans for the weekend?" We were chatting recently about a friend of ours whose mother asks what that daughter considers too many questions. When I commented on my conscious practice of not asking many questions, my daughter said, "I actually wish you would ask me more." When (in total surprise) I asked why, she said, "I want to know you are interested in me." God is interested in us. By

God cares about the practical side of life and about us as individuals.

telling us to pray daily about what we need, Jesus affirms that God is interested in all that concerns us; our prayers about mundane matters indicate our trust in that fact.

YOURS, MINE, AND OURS

This prayer petition, however, is not solely personal. Jesus did not suggest praying, "Give me my daily bread." As in the beginning of the prayer, by saying "our," Jesus sets the life of prayer within community. In the same way, concern for daily needs to be met does not stop at our own door, which seems especially true in light of the world's food shortages today.

A pastor in New England decided to illustrate for her congregation the global situation with food and hunger. She invited the congregation to a meal, setting up three tables to represent the people of the world. The number of chairs at each table represented the percentage of Earth's people who live in the circumstances symbolized by the food on that table. On one table sat a small cup of water and one "survival biscuit"—emergency rations. The second table bore a pot of soup, mostly chicken broth, along with small bowls and a container of water. The most chairs circled this table. A damask tablecloth covered the third table, which was set with silver, china, and a five-course meal, including a fancy dessert. The fewest chairs surrounded this table. A small boy seated at the third table looked around him and said, "This isn't fair! If Jesus were here, he'd do something about it." That little boy seemed to understand a great deal about Jesus and about fairness.

The disparity in the world's food supply and other wealth isn't fair. Those of us who live in rich, industrialized nations have far more of almost everything than we need. Obesity is a national epidemic in the U.S., while many people in other places starve. (There are hungry people in the U.S. too, but on the whole, the food supply surpasses that in many countries.) In recent years, food use and production around the world have shifted. People are eating more meat; animals raised for food are now being fattened on grains that formerly fed people directly. Both floods and droughts interfere with agriculture,

Week 3

and uneven distribution of the food that's available leaves many unable to buy what they need at a reasonable price.

So when we pray "Give us this day our daily bread," we are acknowledging again that we are in this life together. When we claim kinship with God, we claim kinship with God's children as well. And if we start praying for others, we usually will find ourselves nudged to do more than pray. If we pray "Give us this day our daily bread" as genuine intercession for those with nothing or too little to eat, in time our awareness of their hunger will draw us into other, more concrete responses.

LIVING GOD'S PRIORITIES

Numerous scripture passages describe God's desire to care for the hungry and the poor. In Leviticus God gives instructions to landowners about leaving some produce for the poor to glean from the fields at harvest. Proverbs commends the one who is generous toward those in need. Psalm 12:5 says, "'Because the poor are despoiled, because the needy groan, I will now rise up,' says the LORD, 'I will place them in the safety for which they long.'" Psalm 146:7 praises God as the one who sets prisoners free and "gives food to the hungry."

The New Testament reflects God's concern for the poor as well. The familiar passage in Matthew 25 tells us that when we feed the hungry, visit those sick and in prison, and clothe the naked, it is as if we are doing these acts of charity for the Lord. Once after Jesus had been healing people from the crowd that was following him, the disciples suggested he send the people into nearby villages so they could buy food. But Jesus said instead, "You give them something to eat" (Matt. 14:16). The disciples looked at one another, and one said, "But Lord—we don't have anything to feed so many!" Or something like that. Jesus said, "You give them something to eat." (What happens next is the miracle we usually call the feeding of the five thousand.)

We might prefer that God take care of others' needs directly, with a miracle, or that God send an angel and not ask us to get involved. But Jesus said, "Give them something to eat." We also are called to respond to the world's needs, in the midst of our daily routines.

ARE YOU THE ANSWER?

Some years ago, I went out later than usual one Sunday night to walk my dog, closing the door firmly behind me. At the end of our walk, I looked down to discover I was carrying not my house keys but my car keys. We were locked out. A night-owl neighbor and I tried for almost an hour to get into my house. It became obvious that I would either have to call a locksmith or retrieve the spare key to my house from a friend living across town. I decided that the drive would be cheaper than a locksmith.

As I was driving home, I passed a girl about fourteen or fifteen years old, walking toward me. The semi-rural area had few houses along this stretch of road. By this time it was almost midnight, and I was concerned that she was not safe. Offering rides to strangers or accepting rides is not usually wise, and so I passed her by. But I had a strong urging, almost a physical ache in my chest, that I should help her. I turned my car around. Pulling up alongside her, I put down the window and said, "I shouldn't be offering and you shouldn't be accepting, but do you need a ride somewhere?"

"If I could just get to a telephone . . ." I opened the door and motioned for her to get in. When she sat down next to me, I could see her trembling. She turned her head to speak to me, and I looked into her eyes. At that moment I had a clear sense of something I had never experienced before. Almost as if a voice were speaking, I sensed inwardly, "You are the answer to someone's prayer for this girl." The clarity of the impression gave me goose bumps. I took the girl to a nearby store and asked the security guard there to keep an eye on her until someone came for her.

As I drove home, thinking about what had just happened, I felt sure God was at work in the circumstances of that night. I don't mean God caused me to lock myself out; I don't believe God works that way. God did not send that teenager into a bad situation. And it wasn't God or an angel who turned my car around either; it was me. But I would not usually have been driving in that area at that hour, just as that young girl would not usually be walking there, and I remain convinced that God used my situation to answer someone's prayer for that young woman.

God calls everybody to do something, but God doesn't call anybody to do everything.

Week 3

A parent or grandparent, an aunt or uncle or cousin, a youth minister, a neighbor, a teacher, a schoolmate—someone who cared—had been praying for her. That person wasn't near and able to help, but I was.

I've thought about that incident many times, wondering how it would affect our lives if we went into our days willing to pay attention to and act on the inner nudges we sense when we encounter need. As those who are hungry pray for food and we pray for God to give "daily bread," our eyes can be opened to see opportunities to become part of God's answer to that prayer. All who pray as Jesus taught are part of one community, woven together by the love of God. Within that community, our prayers for daily bread and others' daily actions, and their prayers for daily bread and our actions, are part of a single network. God's power flows within and among all of us, and we all can participate in what God is doing—if we make ourselves available.

EXPRESSIONS OF GOD'S LOVE

We pray not just for daily bread but for all physical needs to be met—for housing and jobs and clean water and all life's other necessities. And praying for these for ourselves leads us naturally into praying the same for others. When we pray, we should not be surprised by continual reminders that we are meant to be the expression of God's care and power in the situations we pray about. We embody God's presence in the world; we are the continuing incarnation of the love of God seen in Christ.

Of course, none of us can or should try to accomplish all that needs to be done. God calls everybody to do something, but God doesn't call anybody to do everything. But we also recognize and honor every effort as an expression of moving this world closer to what God wants it to be. There's an old story about a little boy walking along a beach where thousands of starfish have been stranded as the tide receded. The little boy is picking up one starfish after another and throwing them back out into the water. A man sees him and says, "Son, there are thousands of these starfish. You can't make a difference."

The little boy turns as he finishes launching another starfish back into deep water and says to the man, "I made a difference for that one." We can't help every hungry child in the inner city or provide wells to every village in Africa or send medical supplies to every struggling clinic in Central America. But what we can do, God uses to make a difference.

HUNGRY FOR MORE THAN BREAD

We also know that even when we have what we need physically, our hearts still may not be at rest. We experience vague, inexpressible yearning. At the center of this yearning lies our need to know and be known by God. Jesus said that we do not live by bread alone. Pascal wrote of "the infinite abyss" within each of us that can be filled only by God; Augustine said that our hearts are restless until they find rest in God. This need for God, like physical needs, cannot be satisfied once and for all. Jesus' direction to pray "Give us this day . . ." implies reaching out to God daily. The manna that God provided to the Hebrews in the wilderness was a tangible expression of their daily need for food, but it also made real their daily tie to God.

Our need for connection with God is no less real, though we do not have manna to remind us of that. But we do have other reminders. I work with *The Upper Room* magazine, a daily devotional guide. Each day's devotional includes a suggested reading from scripture, a verse quoted from the Bible, and a brief story tying scripture to life. The story is usually a personal experience. Writers tell how they have seen and felt God's presence and grace in ordinary situations. When magazine staff members travel, we meet many people who identify a particular meditation and then say, "It was exactly what I needed to hear that day," or, "I felt like that meditation was put there just for me."

Recently a woman with an extreme version of that experience approached one of our staff. The woman carried a large, three-ring binder. On each sheet of paper was a copy of a meditation from *The Upper Room*, and on the rest of the page she had written how that day's content—the scripture reading or the quoted verse or some aspect of the writer's story—linked specifically to a situation in her life that day. She said, "I don't see how you all do it, but every single day you publish what I need to hear that day." The woman thought we

This need for God, like physical needs, cannot be satisfied once and for all.

were making this happen; she did not realize that something else was going on. Over time, in reading the scripture every day and placing herself before God, she had learned to recognize God's voice, shown by her making those connections for herself. When we keep looking for God in daily events and asking for God's help and guidance, we learn to see the many ways God shows up in our lives (often in a surprising disguise) and to recognize God's voice.

Every day God comes to us. Every day God waits for us to pray in gratitude and trust, asking for what we and what others need. Some days we ask for courage, some days for healing, some days for the ability to love, some days for food and clothing, some days for strength to get through a challenge we'd prefer not to face. And God who hears our honest prayers responds. There's much that is sacred in every day, and through these abundant small miracles God calls our name, asking us to pay attention. Praying for and offering "daily bread" is one way we show God that we are listening.

———◆•◆———

WEEK 3 DAILY EXAMEN

Before you get out of bed in the morning or before you fall asleep at night, look back over the preceding twenty-four hours. Then think about this:

How did God feed me? How did I feed others?

———◆•◆———

DAILY SCRIPTURE READING AND REFLECTION

Day 1: Read 1 Samuel 1:9-16.

1 Have you ever poured out your heart to God, asking for something you deeply desired? If so, what was the issue? If you have not called out to God in this way, what matters to you enough that you might? What did you—or would you—ask for?

2 How does this passage make you feel and think about praying?

3 Who has talked to you about prayer or modeled for you how to pray? What did you learn from this person/these people?

Week 3

Day 2: Read Luke 11:5-10.

1 Think about a time when you assisted someone in need. How did it make you feel? What insights came from the experience? How do you think God feels about helping us?

2 What have you asked God for many times? Why do you keep asking?

3 What gifts in your life do you credit directly to God's generosity toward you, personally?

Day 3: Read Psalm 63:1, 6-8.

1 Remember an occasion when you were very thirsty, such as after being in the sun for a long time. In what situations have you been aware of a spiritual thirst or emptiness that you identify as yearning to know God? If you have not felt that, would you want to, and if so, why?

2 What satisfies your spiritual hunger and thirst?

3 Are you more apt to "meditate" or think deeply about God in "the watches of the night" or at some other time of day?

Day 4: Read Luke 11:11-13.

1 What is the best gift you have ever received? Who was the giver, and what was the occasion? What's the best gift you have ever given, and why?

2 What feelings or thoughts come to you when you consider asking God for specific material help or outcomes? Do you ask?

3 Have you ever received a specific answer to a request you made of God? What was the situation and the answer? If not, how do you respond when others describe receiving specific answers to prayer?

Day 5: Read Mark 2:2-5, 9-12.

1 Close your eyes and, using your imagination, place yourself in this story. Which character are you—the one on the pallet, one of the four carrying it, or one in the crowd? Why are you this character?

2 Who needs you to "carry" them into Christ's presence? In addition to praying, how might you do this? Who would you call on to carry you into Christ's presence, and why?

3 Jesus did not address this man's obvious need first. What does this say to you about how we pray for others?

PREPARING FOR YOUR GROUP MEETING

If you have time to look back over your daily reflection pages, think about these questions:

Did you do daily examen? If so, what's your response to the practice? Did it change you or your actions?

Which of the week's scripture passages seemed particularly appropriate to something you were concerned about?

What in this week's readings most challenged or surprised you?

MEETING NOTES/RESPONSES

WE'RE GOOD PEOPLE

Forgive us our sins.

—ᴗᴖᴖ—

Almighty God, . . . We acknowledge and bewail our manifold sins and wickedness, which we from time to time most grievously have committed, by thought, word, and deed, against thy divine majesty. We do earnestly repent, and are heartily sorry for these our misdoings; the remembrance of them is grievous unto us. Have mercy upon us, have mercy upon us, most merciful [God]. For thy Son our Lord Jesus Christ's sake, forgive us all that is past.

—THE UNITED METHODIST HYMNAL[1]

Sunday worship had included Holy Communion. As the congregants were leaving, many shook hands with the preacher and exchanged pleasantries. But one longtime member stopped to declare vehemently, "I just hate those horrible prayers of confession you make us pray before Communion! Saying we're such sinners and all that—we're not like that here! We're nice people, good people, and I want you to stop making us say those awful things."

What would you have said in response to that woman? The truth is, we are sinners, all of us. *Christian* is not a synonym for *nice* or *polite* or *well brought up. Christian* means we have gone from death to new life. Karl Barth wrote, "To be saved does not just mean to be a little encouraged, a little comforted, a little relieved. It means to be pulled out like a log from a burning fire."[2] We might prefer to think of sin as the little faults and foibles that inconvenience us "good people" and make us feel uncomfortable. Certainly we'd prefer not to have to acknowledge the darkness of the human heart—the darkness of our own heart when we are at our worst. We shrink back from the truth that apart from God's forgiveness, we are headed for spiritual death. That's not a pleasant prospect—and most of us want pleasant lives.

MAKING LIGHT OF SIN

We'd prefer to picture sin as something outside of us and to make light of human wrongs. Years ago while visiting West Virginia Wesleyan University, I noticed an interesting item posted on the religion department's bulletin board. The pseudo–final exam for a religion course featured an "essay question" that read: "Choose and describe your personal favorite of the seven deadly sins. Explain your reasoning."

These seven deadly sins—greed, lust, gluttony, envy, pride, anger, and sloth (apathy)—are called mortal ("deadly") because in Roman Catholic theology, persisting in them will cause us to lose our souls. Making light of sin in the way the "final exam" did is an engaging deception that can keep us from seeing ourselves clearly and naming our sinful behaviors for what they are. C. S. Lewis's book *The Screwtape Letters* touches on the dangers of this way of thinking. Screwtape, an experienced demon, writes a series of letters to his nephew Wormwood, a demon-in-training. In each letter, Screwtape offers pointers about strategies to use in distracting a new believer from maturing in the Christian life. One strategy Screwtape recommends to Wormwood is getting the new Christian to minimize sins. If Wormwood can convince his target that he is all right as he is, the new Christian will not need to cooperate in God's work of transformation.

Some sins do not seem immediately dangerous. Stealing pens from the office is certainly not on the same level of moral depravity or harm to others as sexual abuse or murder. But all sin is still sin, and we cannot remove even its tiniest stain from our souls. Nor can we undo the effect of even our smallest wrongdoing on others. That's why we need help from outside ourselves, why we need to be saved from sin and what it does to us.

THE UGLY TRUTH

One of the ugliest stories in the Bible is the rarely told account of Herod's actions after Jesus is born. Though its brutality makes it painful to read, the story demonstrates our need for a savior. After hearing the Magi's story about the baby born to be a king, Herod is "frightened, and all Jerusalem with him" (Matt. 2:3). That indicates something of what the people of Jerusalem already knew about Herod. The threatened king becomes furious because the Magi have gone home without telling him where to find Jesus, so he sends his agents to kill "all the children in and around Bethlehem who were two years old or under" (Matt. 2:16). This gruesome event is called the "Slaughter of the Innocents," and the liturgical calendar marks the event on Holy Innocents' Day. Our stories and images of a sweet baby Jesus are jarred by this horrible act.

Sin destroys us; that's why God hates it.

What does this disturbing story say to us about our sin? It tells us that sin is ugly and destructive. Sin destroys us; that's why God hates it. And that's why God forgives our sin and woos us away from it—because God does not want us to be destroyed. The Gospel of John says, "God so loved the world that he gave his only begotten son." Jesus' death was the price of our salvation. "For God is not willing that any should perish but that all should come to repentance" (John 3:17). That's why Jesus reminds us to make sin a matter of prayer—because though we cannot remove our sin, God can and will when we ask.

THE SINNER IN THE MIRROR

Here is the issue we face in our reluctance to confess that we have sinned: to do so acknowledges that we need God's help—and we don't want to admit that. The flip side of the love of power is hatred of—or at least contempt for—our own neediness and sometimes even

Week 4

the neediness of others. We want to live in the delusion that we are strong. Lines like "I am the master of my fate: I am the captain of my soul" appeal to our individualism. But writer Emmet Fox comments in his interpretation of the Lord's Prayer that our "belief in independent and separate existence is the arch sin."[3] In other words, saying we don't need God is the insult at the core of our arrogance.

SHADES OF SIN

What is sin, anyway? Several different words are translated into English as "sin" in the Bible. In Hebrew Scripture (the Old Testament), words meaning in Hebrew "to offend" or "to bear guilt" are both translated as *sin*. Another word translated "sin" means more exactly, in Hebrew, rebellion or going against what is right; a fourth means to wander astray from the path or to be enraptured by something and drawn away.

The New Testament talks about sin in various ways: as missing the mark (like an archer aiming at a target) or falling short, as consciously choosing to do something that offends God or hurts another person, and as straying unintentionally from the path God asks us to follow. Regardless of which comparison we use or which way we sin, all of us fail, and all of us need forgiveness for it.

The Bible offers only one remedy: repenting and asking God to forgive us. But the repentance that the Bible commends is not an exercise in self-hatred and condemnation, what I call "worm theology"— "for such a wretch as I," as if we are worthless and unredeemable. That characterization does not reflect God's view of us. To God, each one of us is worth the death of Jesus; Jesus died to bring us to repentance and new life. One of the New Testament epistles makes a distinction between "godly sorrow"—regret and sadness about our sin—and "earthly sorrow" (KJV). Godly sorrow leads to repentance, forgiveness, and life; earthly sorrow—castigating ourselves, focusing on how bad we are and going no further—leads not to life but to death (2 Cor. 7:9, 10).

A CHANGE OF DIRECTION

Coming to know Christ and committing to follow Christ do not mean that we will no longer sin. If this were the case, Jesus would not have included asking forgiveness in his outline for our praying. The repentance that brings us into saving relationship with Christ does not guarantee instant and permanent moral cleansing and completely changed personality and behavior.

To "repent" means literally to "think again." (Vocabulary lesson: The prefix re- means again, as in "return," "repeat," "reread," etc.; the root word -pent comes from the Latin root word penser, "to think." The same root appears in the word pensive, which means "thoughtful" or "lost in thought.") Another Greek word also translated "repent" means to change course, to turn in a different direction.

So when we repent, we change our mind, our overall direction, our destination. Think of it this way: When we decide to go to Florida for a beach vacation, we head south. The first turn south does not get us to Florida instantly, but we will never get there if we don't begin moving in that direction. Following Christ and becoming like Christ is a journey that begins with changing our minds, changing the direction of our lives. Then gradually, over time, God changes our hearts and our behavior as well. (See Rom. 12:1-2 and 2 Cor. 3:16-18.)

In spite of our commitment to follow Christ—or perhaps because we do not like being reminded of our failure to keep that commitment—we find it hard to admit to ourselves and others that we have sinned. Having someone else point out our sin to us is even worse. In the movie *You've Got Mail*, Kathleen (Meg Ryan) stands up and leaves her boyfriend, Frank (Greg Kinnear), in a movie theater after he says, "I forgive you." She does not believe she needs his forgiveness, and his judgment of her and presumption in implying that she has sinned makes her angry.

We don't want to need forgiveness. Asking forgiveness requires us to humble ourselves, to acknowledge that we've done something wrong. When we ask to be forgiven, we place ourselves in a position where another has power over us. The person we have harmed can

"Forgive us our sins" is one prayer that . . . will always be answered.

Week 4

affect our feelings and our future; most of us don't like that kind of vulnerability.

But we can be comforted by the knowledge that asking God's forgiveness is easier than asking another person to forgive us because God forgives more readily than people ever will. The Bible assures us repeatedly that God is both able and willing to forgive us and to restore us: "If you, O LORD, should mark iniquities, Lord, who could stand? But there is forgiveness with you. . . . with the LORD there is steadfast love, and with him is great power to redeem" (Ps. 130:3-4, 7). "Bless the LORD, O my soul, and forget not all his benefits—who forgives all your iniquity" (Ps. 103:2-3). "Everyone who believes in [Jesus Christ] receives forgiveness of sins through his name" (Acts 10:43). "If we confess our sins, [God] who is faithful and just to forgive us our sins and to cleanse us from all unrighteousness" (1 John 1:9). We can trust God's unfailing forgiveness. In fact, "Forgive us our sins" is one prayer that we can know will always be answered.

THE LAST HURDLE

Other people usually will forgive us. God always will. We need forgiveness from one more party: ourselves. Forgiving ourselves can be the most difficult hurdle we face. At least I know it is for me.

Recently I behaved badly toward another person. At the end of a particularly difficult day at the office—dealing with technology and with people—I stopped for a haircut at my usual salon. The next evening I would emcee an event in front of a large group, so I asked the hairdresser to give me just the slightest trim. I cautioned her repeatedly not to cut off much, and she assured me repeatedly that she was just trimming—but I left with hair so short I could not curl or style it. I was upset!

I stopped at a service station nearby to put gasoline in my car, intending to pay at the pump with a charge card. I inserted my card and removed it "quickly," as the display on the pump instructed me. The screen went blank. I swiped my card several more times, but the pump would not work. I finally went inside the store—which I had been trying to avoid by paying at the pump. When I told the clerk about my problem at the pump and gave her its number, she said the kind of thing that infuriates me at such gas stations: "Pumps seven and eight have been acting up all day." To me, those words proved that the inconvenience and frustration I was experiencing could have been prevented. I said—angrily—"I would appreciate it very much if you would put a note on the pump saying so when that happens. Then I could go to another pump. The object of using my card is to avoid having to come inside." Rack up one deadly sin for me: anger.

"Oh, I can take care of it here. How much do you want?"

"I don't know how much I want; I was intending to fill up." I made a wild stab at an amount. When she tried to authorize that amount on pump number eight, she could not.

"I'll just go to this other register," she said. I followed her to another checkout counter. She could not get the pump to accept my purchase from that register either—several times. Meanwhile, a line of customers was building up behind me, and I was building up even more frustration and anger.

I said to her, "Look, I am having a very bad day. I've just been scalped by the hairdresser, and this is not helping." Finally I snatched my card from her hand and said, "Just forget it. I don't have time for this!" And I headed for the door. I had not said anything about her personally, but I was impatient and angry toward someone who was simply trying to do her job—and in front of several people. As I left the parking lot, I was overwhelmed with shame at how I had acted in the store.

Reflecting on what had just happened, I asked myself what was at the root of my behavior. Instantly I recognized that another of the seven deadly sins, vanity (pride), had set me off. That makes two of the seven deadlies. I don't usually consider myself a vain person; I hate fooling with makeup and do the absolute minimum. But as I have gotten older my hair has become thin and very difficult to manage. I was upset about how I would look the next night. I envy my mother's thick, coarse, curly hair. Envy—that makes three. I was deeply disappointed in how I had acted. Berating myself, I said inwardly, "Mary Lou, you should be more patient and gentle. You are beyond behaving like

Week 4

that." Again—pride, and in my opinion the worse kind, spiritual pride. I had managed to commit three deadly sins during one incident. (I strive to be efficient, no matter what I'm doing—even sinning.)

Throughout the evening, self-recrimination immobilized me. I kept replaying in my mind the incident with the clerk. At bedtime I took time to write in my journal about my day and about how badly I had behaved. I asked God to forgive me for my sin and to help me be the person I know God wants me to be. But I still felt terrible—ashamed and sad that I am still so weak and sinful after all my years of following Christ.

As I drove to work the next morning, still preoccupied with memories of the previous afternoon, God said in my heart, "Do you believe that I forgive you when you ask?" I said that of course I did. And God said in my heart, "So I forgive you, but don't you have to forgive yourself?" I understood that God was nudging me to let go of my sin and my self-centeredness about it. "There is one condition for receiving God's gift of forgiveness," wrote Douglas Steere. "[We] must be willing to accept it." Steere continued:

> [F]ew . . . will believe in and accept the forgiveness of God so completely as to . . . leave their sin with God forever. They are always opening the vault where they have deposited their sin, . . . forever asking to have it back in order to fondle it; reconstruct, query, or worry over it.[4]

Clinging to our sin once we have asked forgiveness is an affront to God's generosity and grace. God offers us forgiveness every day—because we need it every day for the sins we commit by our actions, and for the sins we commit by not acting.

"For freedom Christ has set us free," says the epistle to the Galatians. "[Do] not submit again to a yoke of slavery" (5:1). God invites us to acknowledge and repent of our sins not in order to feel bad about ourselves but in order to receive forgiveness, be freed, and become whole. The forgiveness God offers and willingly gives sets us on the road to joyful obedience.

Week 4

BUT WAIT—THERE'S MORE

Like other portions of the Lord's Prayer, this petition is not limited to individuals. Jesus said, "Forgive us *our* sins," reminding us again that we live within community. Communities sin and need to be redeemed. Whether we are talking about huge and universally denounced sins, such as abuse of children by clergy, or our quieter sins of prejudice, exclusiveness, and judgment, the community of those who follow Christ needs our prayers. Our unity in Christ has also been fractured and threatened by theological disputes. We call one another names and even question one another's commitment to Christ because of political differences. We need forgiveness for our sins, and we need healing.

One of the guided prayers we use within a community I'm part of leads us through praying for a succession of groups: ourselves individually, the community gathered, those who are part of the community but absent from us, our city and its leaders, our state, our nation, the world. The Bible tells us that God loves the world—and the word used in John 3:16 means not just people but the cosmos, the entire created order. In many ways we harm one another and this world that God loves.

The prophets call us to work and pray for a different world than we have. Micah envisions a time when the faithful will beat swords into plowshares and spears into pruning hooks (4:3)—that is, take weapons of war that can end life and instead make them into tools that help to support life. That same verse speaks of a time when we will not "learn war any more." But we continue fighting. As I write this, more than thirty armed conflicts rage around the globe, killing both military personnel and civilians.[5] War destroys entire cities and creates orphans and refugees. Isaiah calls us to feed the poor, but hunger grows at an alarming rate (58:1-12). Amos calls us to work for justice (5:24), but still we tolerate racial divides and discrimination against people based on religious faith, national identity, and ethnic heritage.

The world needs people who will "stand in the gap" (Ezek. 22:30), who will intercede for all our global needs and sins, trusting

"For freedom Christ has set us free."—Gal. 5:1

Week 4

and inviting God to work in this world that God loves so much. The model for prayer that Jesus taught us opens the door to that possibility, every day.

———◆·◆———

WEEK 4 DAILY EXAMEN

Before you get out of bed in the morning or before you fall asleep at night, look back over the preceding twenty-four hours. Then think about this:

Where did I sense God's grace and forgiveness?

———◆·◆———

Week 4

DAILY SCRIPTURE READING AND REFLECTION

Day 1: Read Ezekiel 11:14, 17-20.

1 In the last few days has your heart been more a "heart of stone" or a "heart of flesh"? What makes you say this?

2 What has God done to bring you back when you have wandered or been "scattered"? How or in whom have you experienced God's love seeking you?

3 In what ways or situations would you like God to give you a new heart and a new spirit? How would you be different once you had this new heart?

Week 4

Day 2: Read Psalm 51:1-4, 17 and Isaiah 6:7.

1 Where do you struggle repeatedly to do what you know God wants? When you fail, are you able to let go of guilt about wrong acts you've confessed and repented of, or is your sin "ever before [you]"? What helps you to feel forgiven?

2 Take two minutes to think about God's steadfast love and God's mercy. Then list the words you associate with these two qualities. Who has demonstrated these qualities to you? What did that person or those persons do?

3 Put yourself into Isaiah 6:7: "My guilt has departed and my sin is blotted out." Repeat that sentence a few times and then sit quietly. What inner response are you aware of? What do you want to say to God about this?

Day 3: Read 1 John 1:5-9.

1 Sit in a darkened room or close your eyes and think about what it means to be filled with light. What does light bring with it? Where do you need light this week?

2 What does it mean to "walk in the light"? How can we tell if someone is walking in the light?

3 Under what conditions can we confess our sins? What do you need in order to be able to confess? What does it mean to you to know that God is faithful in forgiving sin?

Day 4: Read Romans 7:21–8:2. (Start at 7:14 if time allows.)

1 How do you experience the struggle between the rebellious part of yourself and the part that wants to follow God? Does "war" describe the process accurately for you? Why? If not, with what would you compare your inner struggle?

2 Have you ever felt condemned? Where does this feeling come from? Does admitting failures and sins make you feel worse or better about yourself? Why confess sin?

3 Do you forgive yourself as you would a repentant friend who stumbles or "trespasses"? How do you think God wants you to treat yourself?

Week 4

Day 5: Read Matthew 18:12-13.

1 Have you more often been one of the ninety-nine who stay or the one who strays? How do you think people in the two groups experience and respond to forgiveness differently?

2 Sit quietly for at least a minute and picture God "rejoicing over" you. Allow God to hold you. How does this affect your ideas about forgiveness? What do you want to say to God?

3 Based on this passage, who initiates the process of our being forgiven? Do you "feel" forgiven? How do our feelings figure into forgiving and being forgiven?

PREPARING FOR YOUR GROUP MEETING

If you have time to look back over your daily reflection pages, think about these questions:

Did you do daily examen? If so, what's your response to the practice? Did it change you or your actions?

Which of the week's scripture passages seemed particularly appropriate to something you were concerned about?

What in this week's readings most challenged or surprised you?

MEETING NOTES/RESPONSES

The Ultimate Two-Way Street

Forgive us, . . . as we also have forgiven our debtors.

———

Clean White Boxes

I closed a feeling up
in a clean, slick, white box
and put it on a shelf,
then gently closed the closet door.
I held the cool gray keys to all the locks
and hugged them to myself.

Each
time I'd
add a box I'd note
how straight and neat
the stacks were growing as
the feelings mounted up within
my tiny, quiet, safe, and tidy cell.

But one day I made up
an ordinary box—pedestrian, austere—
and when I put it on the shelf,
the whole mess fell

around me—
a heap of old, old feelings
rancid, moldy, bitter,
that had spoiled for being hidden.

Like manna,
feelings do not keep well.[1]

—MARY LOU REDDING[1]

About twenty years ago I was in an auto accident. The driver of an eighteen-wheeler who was not paying attention hit my car from behind. I sustained an assortment of injuries, and because of them I live with chronic pain of varying intensity. After the accident, I fell into the habit of referring to the driver of the truck as "that jerk Abraham Lincoln"—especially when I was in pain. (I used his real name, but—big surprise—that is not it.)

Usually the pain remains at a level I can ignore, but for some reason, traveling always makes it worse. One blustery day about ten years ago, I was on a business trip that took me through Chicago. I flew into Midway Airport and had to take a shuttle to O'Hare, the other Chicago airport, to connect with my next flight. The shuttle was supposed to run every twenty minutes. By the time I got to Midway late in the day I was already in considerable pain, and after standing at the shuttle stop for more than thirty minutes in the cold, I was truly miserable. As the wind whipped my coat around me, I said to God, "Well, God, here I am, hurting again. And I'll bet that jerk Abraham Lincoln never even thinks about that accident. He just walked away. He suffered no consequences, and I'm standing here all these years later, still in pain, feeling like I could cry . . ."

God interrupted me with one of the holy-sounding messages that characterize how I hear the Divine: "Don't you think it's about time you forgave that guy and moved on?" I immediately answered with a resounding internal no. Sneering his name to God made me feel better, thank you very much, and I was not interested in forgiving him.

But on reflection, it seemed wise to me to at least consider God's suggestion. Eventually I told God that though I did not want to forgive old "Abe," I was willing to be made willing. I prayed for God's help to change my attitude. I wrote in my journal about my experience at the airport, acknowledged that perhaps I needed to consider forgiving the man who had caused me so much grief, and put the incident out of my mind. A good while later, perhaps eighteen months or two years down the road, the subject of the long-ago accident came up in conversation with a friend. I started to refer to the driver with my standard "that jerk _____"—and I could not recall his name! No one could have been more surprised than I was. Looking back, I also realized that in the preceding months I had experienced less pain from those old injuries than was typical.

Was there a connection between my prayer for help in forgiving and my having less pain? I don't know. But I know that after I prayed for God's help to forgive, the driver and the accident took up less emotional space in my life than they had in years. These days I still hurt because of those old injuries, sometimes a lot, but the pain doesn't propel me back into reliving my resentment the way I was that day at the airport.

Forgiving runs counter to what our culture expects and teaches.

LIMITING FORGIVENESS

When Jesus told us to pray for forgiveness, he tied that request to a responsibility on our part: "as we also have forgiven our debtors." The familiar wording "as we forgive those who trespass against us" perhaps captures that element better for us. We are to forgive those whose behavior hurts or has hurt us in the past. This link suggests a curious possibility: that we limit experiencing God's forgiveness ourselves if we refuse to forgive others. Though we may say that God is sovereign and can do anything, apparently this is not so; we experience forgiveness only to the extent that we offer it.

Why did Jesus suggest that we make forgiving others a matter of prayer? Because forgiving is tough. Forgiveness is not cheap. It costs us something, just as our forgiveness cost Jesus dearly. Forgiveness often is less an event than it is a process. Because forgiving runs counter to what our culture expects and teaches, forgiving witnesses to God's power.

As my experience with "Abraham Lincoln" shows, we don't have to forgive. God does not force us to forgive. In fact, some of us have multiple, well-developed strategies to avoid forgiving. A story from Hebrew Scripture shows several of the strategies we use—and some of the consequences of not forgiving. Found in the book of Second Samuel, chapters 13–19, this complicated, long story involves Tamar, Absalom, Amnon, and their father, King David.

Here's a summary: Amnon falls in love with his beautiful half sister, Tamar. He tricks her into coming to his bedroom and rapes her. Tamar leaves, having torn her clothing in distress. She tells her brother Absalom what has happened. He replies, "Don't be upset," but he is furious and plots revenge. Two years later Absalom and his servants kill Amnon, and Tamar remains in Absalom's home, "desolate."

King David, rather than facing the actions of his sons and the crime against his daughter, banishes Absalom (instead of executing him). Eventually Joab, another relative, schemes to get Absalom back to Jerusalem, though Absalom and his father do not speak for two years after Absalom returns. Eventually Absalom mounts a rebellion to overthrow his father. But Absalom dies in battle, and the whole affair ends in one of the saddest scenes in all of scripture, with David pacing the walls of his palace, crying, "O my son Absalom, O Absalom, my son, my son!" in grief for loss of his son—only a part of his loss of relationships in the family.

INSTEAD OF FORGIVING

This story shows us several classic strategies in not forgiving. (1) Absalom minimizes what happens to his sister. When we are hurt but don't want to confront the one who has injured us, we may say to ourselves and others, "Well, it's really not all that bad. I'll just overlook it. They probably didn't mean it." Or we quote some platitude: "What does not kill us makes us stronger." (2) Tamar retreats. We avoid the one who has hurt us, though we often remain sad and perhaps feel desolate. But we never forget the wrong that's been done. In fact, past hurt can come to define who we are if we hold on tightly to it. (3) Absalom plots and exacts revenge, as we sometimes do, talking behind the scenes and working to retaliate against the one who has hurt us, even pulling in helpers. We may sabotage family members or coworkers in small and big ways, trying to make them miserable because we are miserable. (4) David's first response is denial. He simply closes his eyes to what is going on, as if nothing is wrong. If we don't talk about the bad stuff, it isn't real, and we don't have to do anything about it. This extremely popular strategy actually amounts to lying. Apparently we think lies create less trouble for us than honesty. (5) David banishes the wrongdoer—as we sometimes banish our hurt, sending it to a metaphorical "far country," suppressing it, refusing to talk about it, trying to forget it. But unresolved hurts do not go away. They simmer, growing stronger and more dangerous. We see this in Absalom, whose anger became hatred and rebellion during his exile. And, finally, (6) Joab tinkers. We read in 2 Samuel 14–15 how he manipulates the family, trying to "fix" their relationships. He schemes to get feuding family members together, assuming that they will kiss and make up or at least call a truce. We don't even need an explanation of that one, do we? We also know that this strategy seldom works.

Hanging on to old hurts ties us to the past.

FLYING BEACH BALLS

In the end, the refusal of David's family to face honestly what has happened, acknowledge their pain, and forgive one another results in the family's destruction. Sometimes we simply don't want to do the emotional and relational work that comes with facing our wounds and others' sins—and God does not force us to try. But hanging on to old hurts ties us to the past. Instead of having our energy available to deal with the current day and its concerns, we have to use substantial amounts of energy to baby sit feelings attached to long-ago events.

Years ago I heard writer and speaker Keith Miller compare unresolved past hurts to an inflated beach ball. Miller reminded us that is possible to hold one of those beach balls underwater, but it takes concentration and both hands to do so. In an emotional sense, many of us hold beach balls filled with hurt under the water of superficial peace. Some of us do this extremely well. But when a current situation demands so much attention that we are forced to take one

Week 5

metaphorical hand off of the beach ball, what happens? The ball comes flying out of the water, hitting innocent bystanders who never saw it coming. If we're really lucky, it may hit the person we're angry with—who of course deserves it and had it coming. And if we're really, really lucky, that family member or friend is wearing a very expensive garment that's dry-clean-only.

Forgiveness is our means to deflate the emotional beach balls that take our attention away from today. We can choose to forgive old and new hurts. When we do, we free ourselves to live more fully for God in the present—in our "this day."

WHAT FORGIVENESS IS NOT

We may hold back from forgiving because doing so seems to suggest that someone's hurtful behavior does not matter. Actually, however, forgiving says the opposite. Forgiving starts with acknowledging that we have been hurt and that the person who hurt us has done something wrong. If the action were not wrong, we would not need to forgive. Forgiving says, "What you did was hurtful and unacceptable to me and to God, but I choose to release you from the penalty you deserve." Forgiving makes our failures specific and public, as it does our responsiveness to God's work within and among us.

But sometimes we hold back from forgiving because we don't want to upset others by bringing our hurt out into the open. We may settle for surface tranquility where no one raises a voice or cries. But "peace at any price" often comes with a hefty price tag of simmering hurt and distrust. We may also hold back from forgiving because we want to punish the one who has hurt us. Giving another the cold shoulder allows us to simultaneously be a victim and exact revenge. We do so enjoy a good grudge! However, the old saying about anger "eating at" us offers truth here. Often the person who hurt us moves on into the future, untouched by our emotions, sometimes without even realizing that we've been hurt by their actions. But we continue to harm ourselves by harboring anger that gnaws at us spiritually and emotionally. God offers us a way out.

Week 5

Starting the Process

If we want to be free of life's hurts, God offers us the choice and the gift of being able to forgive. Forgiving an offense can be relatively easy if the hurt is not too great. But when we have been hurt deeply and repeatedly, forgiveness becomes not a one-time action but a journey—and sometimes a long one. Again, this shows Jesus' wisdom in telling us to pray about it.

The process of forgiving asks us to be patient with others and with ourselves. Jesus said that we are to forgive each other "seventy times seven" times (or "seventy-seven times" in some Bible translations—either way, the meaning is "forgive over and over again"). Why do we need to forgive repeatedly? First, because unfortunately, failing one another is a chronic problem in relationships. Even when we don't intend harm, we offend and wound others. As long as we are human, we will need to forgive and to ask others to forgive us.

Jesus' seventy-times-seven admonition can also have another meaning. When we have been deeply hurt, we may discover that we have to forgive someone over and over again for a single action as we realize new effects of what they did to us. I have learned this from my own experience. My father was an abusive man. When I decided to forgive him, I began first with forgiving him for the literal, physically abusive acts, which was no small task. As time went on, I realized that my relationship with him had led to unhealthy ways of relating to people on my part—so I had to forgive him for teaching me those troublesome patterns of relating. Further along the road, I realized that his emotional abuse had caused an inability to love myself, so I had to forgive him for that. Then I realized that his abuse had caused me to chronically doubt myself and therefore limited my ability to try new things. The harm he inflicted affected me even in something so apparently unrelated as feeling confident in my job, and I had to forgive that. Still further on, I realized that my difficulty in seeing and trusting God as a loving parent was rooted in how my dad treated me, and I had to forgive him again. And so it went—"seventy times seven," layer after layer of hurt—and healing.

Forgiving starts with acknowledging that we have been hurt.

Week 5

GOING AGAINST THE GRAIN

Choosing to forgive someone who has hurt us is countercultural. "Don't get mad; get even" is practically a byword in our society. When we choose to forgive, people may think we are weak. "They had it coming" seems justification for all sorts of behavior. People may even become angry when others choose to forgive.

When we choose to forgive, people may think we are weak.

Several years ago, a woman named Sue Norton chose to forgive a terrible wrong. Her beloved stepfather who had reared her, the man she called "Daddy," was murdered. His killer was apprehended, tried, and convicted. Sue thought she would feel relieved when he was sentenced and would find the "closure" that many people speak of. But the sentencing gave her no peace, and anger about the crime continued to disrupt her life. One night she prayed, asking God what to do. She said God spoke simply to her: "You could forgive him." Because she perceived this message so clearly as she prayed, Sue decided to try. She wrote to the man in prison, eventually visiting and befriending him. But Sue's sister could not accept that Sue had befriended the man who had killed their daddy, and the sisters became estranged. People may not understand when we choose to forgive.

But Jesus showed us that this is his way. From the cross Jesus prayed, "Father, forgive them; for they do not know what they are doing." Jesus showed us that we don't have to withhold forgiveness, waiting until someone repents. If we were to require that, we'd never forgive some hurts because some people will never realize or come to regret that their behavior has harmed us.

More and more I believe Jesus' words are true of almost everyone who hurts us. We are all so focused on ourselves and getting to where we need to be, doing what we need to do, that we often take little notice of others. From merging in traffic to getting time with the boss, we may push others aside both literally and figuratively, not realizing that people feel hurt by what we have done.

Rarely, people may recognize how they have been hurtful and even apologize. A 2010 sports story provides a notable example. It had been a remarkable year for baseball pitching. Before 2010, in all of major-league baseball history, only twenty perfect games had been

Week 5

pitched. (A perfect game means no runner got on base: twenty-seven consecutive batters failed to get a base hit, and the pitcher never put anyone on base by throwing four balls.) That year, two perfect games already had been recorded when, in a game between Cleveland and Detroit, pitcher Armando Galarraga seemed about to pitch the third. Multiple sports channels were checking in on the game, interspersing their regular coverage with updates on Galarraga's progress.

In the ninth inning, Galarraga struck out the first two batters and needed only one more out to have his perfect game. Earlier that week, Galarraga had almost been sent back to the minor leagues, so a great deal was at stake for him. Pitching well could save his major-league career. With two outs on the scoreboard, Armando pitched and the batter hit a routine ground ball between first and second base. The first baseman ran over to stop the ball, and Galarraga went to cover first base, as the pitcher is supposed to. He caught the ball well before the runner reached the base, but umpire Jim Joyce called the runner safe. *Sports Illustrated* writer Joe Posnanski commented that Galarraga turned to look at the umpire with a simple smile. That smile seemed to say, "Are you sure? I hope you are really sure." Later, the replay showed clearly what most of the spectators knew, that the umpire had been mistaken. Joyce apologized, which is unheard of for an umpire. Galarraga said that Joyce probably felt worse than he did (I doubt it) and then continued, "Nobody's perfect." But in spite of Joyce's apology and regret, Galarraga was harmed. His amazing feat will not go into the record books except perhaps as a footnote. Galarraga rightly stated our universal imperfection—and that's why we can be thankful for the gift of forgiveness.

FORGIVING THE UNTHINKABLE

Forgiveness is possible in sports settings and in much more difficult, seemingly unthinkable circumstances. You may remember the 2006 tragedy when a gunman named Charles Carl Roberts entered an Amish school in Nickel Mines, Pennsylvania, lined up ten little girls who were students there, and shot them. Three girls died nearly instantly. Then Roberts killed himself as the remaining students

Week 5

watched. The Amish are pacifists; they do not use weapons or participate in armed conflict. They live simple lives, without electricity and television. They are not exposed to the violence pervasive in entertainment and even in daily news reports. Imagine the shock and horror they must have felt.

That night the families in the Amish community gathered to pray for their injured children and to draw strength and comfort from one another. As they struggled with their own grief and loss, they also asked a remarkable question: How could they help the family of the troubled man who shot their children? They already had planned a horse-and-buggy caravan to visit the family, to take them food and offer sympathy for their loss. But they wanted to do more. They wanted to let the family know that they did not hold them responsible. This is the miracle of forgiveness: acknowledging wrong but refusing to punish the wrongdoer. Secular news commentators marveled at the faith of the Amish people of Nickel Mines. That's how remarkable our culture finds forgiving.

Evidence of Forgiveness

In spite of the familiar saying "forgive and forget," forgetting an offense is highly unusual. The normal human brain remembers; that's why amnesia and dementia are classified as medical problems. Although I temporarily forgot that truck driver's name, forgiving does not require forgetting what others have done. The surest evidence of forgiveness is freedom—freedom for the offender and for the one offended. If my stomach still churns when I meet someone who has harmed me, if memories of the past dominate my thoughts, I am not free. The cords of anger or sadness or both bind me to that person. Obviously I have not forgotten my accident, but I also no longer hold it against the driver. That's why his name no longer matters.

Forgiving changes the way we respond both internally and externally to those who have harmed us. For example, a friend of mine always had a difficult time choosing Father's Day cards for her dad. He had been a demanding, gruff, career-military man. The "you're-the-best-dad-in-the-world" Father's Day greeting cards wouldn't work because she wouldn't sign her name to a card when its message did not ring true for her. She had forgiven her dad for the outward acts that had caused her pain and led to her perpetual efforts to earn approval, but she would not lie to him. Every year it was the same.

Several years ago as she stood before the card display, she began praying for help. Suddenly she had an idea: though she would not sign her name to those untrue sweet sentiments, she could acknowledge how her dad had been part of her life and say that she valued him. She decided to write him a letter recounting memories of places and events they had shared. The letter was not gushy or saccharin. She began with her earliest memories of places they had lived and visits with family. Using her school years as a guide, she tried to recall specific events year by year.

She acknowledged their struggles, but inevitably some of her comments were positive—appreciation for his ability to repair things around the house and gratitude for his teaching her to ride a bike. At the end of the letter, she reminded him how deeply they were linked in spite of their differences, and she told him that she loved him. Then she mailed the letter, expecting him to comment. After a few weeks with no response, she called her dad. He told her through tears that he had not responded because he had been so deeply moved by the letter that he was unable to talk about it. The timing of her prayer, her willingness to obey God's nudge, and the conversation with her dad were gifts; her father died before the next Father's Day.

The spiritual and emotional freedom that allows us to see the good in others in spite of the hurts they may have inflicted and to pray honestly and earnestly for God's best for them is sure evidence of forgiveness.

God welcomes our prayers about relationships.

BEYOND FORGIVENESS

Jesus' direction in this part of the Lord's Prayer reminds us that God welcomes our prayers about relationships. Whether we need wisdom in dealing with our teenagers or aging parents or insight to understand and feel compassion toward a troublesome coworker or the will to forgive, coming to God with those concerns is the right course of

Week 5

action. God is interested and willing to help with struggles of all kinds, with every part of life. What matters to us matters to God. Every relationship and every event that concerns us—even the worst things that have happened to us—can become the subject of our prayers.

———◆·◆———

WEEK 5 DAILY EXAMEN

Before you get out of bed in the morning or before you fall asleep at night, look back over the preceding twenty-four hours. Then think about this:

Where did I show God's grace and offer forgiveness?
Where do I need to offer it?

———◆·◆———

Week 5

DAILY SCRIPTURE READING AND REFLECTION

Day 1: Read Matthew 5:23-24 and 6:14-15.

1 Do you think it is possible to end every day with no "leftover" negative feelings or grudges toward others? If so, how do you get there? What would you say to those who answer differently?

2 What do these verses say to you about the practical benefits of forgiving? Besides refusing to forgive, in what other ways may we limit what God is able to do for us and within us?

3 When have you struggled to forgive? What enabled you to move toward forgiving, if you have been able to? Where do you still need to forgive?

Day 2: Read Matthew 18:15-18.

1 Do you respond differently to wrongful acts of believers as compared to those of nonbelievers? Should we? Why do you say this?

2 What has been your experience in going to those who have hurt
you or been hurt by you and seeking to forgive and be forgiven?
Has another person ever refused to forgive you? What can we do
if or when that happens?

3 If you have never talked to others about their hurtful actions
toward you, what has held you back? Is it ever right to ignore the
wrong that others have done? What does God want for us and for
those who mistreat us?

Week 5

Day 3: Read Hebrews 12:14-15.

1 What does "pursue peace" mean to you? Are some people natural peacemakers, and if so, in what ways? Are you one of them? What characterizes peacemakers?

2 How does obtaining "the grace of God" help avoid bitterness? How can the bitterness of one person cause trouble for many?

3 What can we do to prevent bitterness from becoming "rooted"? If bitterness already has taken root, how can we address deep hurts and become able to forgive?

Week 5

Day 4: Read Luke 22:31-34.

1 Jesus says he has prayed for Peter's faith not to fail, yet he also says that Peter will betray him. What does this suggest to you about our prayers for others? What does this tell us about failure, sin, and faith?

2 How might acknowledging our own failures and sins be useful in strengthening our brothers and sisters? Can failures be so used without publicly admitting them and talking about them? Why or why not?

3 Imagine walking on a beach with Jesus and someone who has hurt you. What do you say to the one who hurt you? What does that person say to you? What does Jesus say and do? How does your walk end?

Day 5: Read Ephesians 4:14-15, 25-32.

1 What do you think it means to "speak the truth in love" when someone has hurt us or mistreated us? Why is this act linked with "growing up"? How might the way we talk about others be a gauge of maturity or of immaturity?

2 How or where do people get the idea that being angry is a sin? How can people be angry and yet not sin? What clues to doing that are given in these verses?

3 Forgive "as God in Christ has forgiven you." How have you come to forgiveness? What can you use from your experience to help you in forgiving others?

Preparing for your group meeting

If you have time to look back over your daily reflection pages, think about these questions:

Did you do daily examen? If so, what's your response to the practice? Did it change you or your actions?

Which of the week's scripture passages seemed particularly appropriate to something you were concerned about?

What in this week's readings most challenged or surprised you?

Meeting Notes/Responses

GOING DOWNTOWN

And do not bring us to the time of trial,
but rescue us from the evil one.

—◦◦◦—

We therefore hope, O Lord our God, soon to behold the glory of Your might. Then
will false gods vanish from our hearts, and the world will be perfected under Your
unchallenged rule. And then will all acclaim You as their God,
and, forsaking evil, turn to You alone.

—FROM GATES OF PRAYER[1]

Many years ago I worked for Oral Roberts. One day in a meeting Mr. Roberts told a story about his two younger children, Richard and Roberta, when they were quite small. The two were discussing whether the world really is such a bad place—one of those theological discussions young children engage in surprisingly often. Roberta's position was similar to the "spark of divinity" belief held by the Quakers. Richard leaned more to the side of original sin and total human depravity. At one point five-year-old Roberta said she just really didn't think the world is all that bad. Richard, the worldly wise seven-year-old, responded, "Oh, Roberta, you just haven't been downtown!"

Many of us would prefer never to go "downtown." We'd love to believe that the world and people are all basically good. We'd love to believe that if we do what is right, our lives will go smoothly and nothing terribly bad will happen to us. We'd love to believe that we can avoid confronting temptation and evil. Unfortunately, experience eventually robs all of us of that innocence.

This last petition in the Lord's Prayer reminds us that Jesus did not shrink from looking at the world and people honestly. For this section, I find the traditional wording "Lead us not into temptation, but deliver us from evil" more fruitful for discussion of our praying. Temptation and the evils that give rise to it are real, and Jesus encourages us to bring this troubling truth into our praying, just as we do our needs and failures. We need not deny and run from our conflicts (inner and outer ones); we are invited to talk with God about them. Christ walks with us through the world that actually exists, not through the world as we wish for it to be.

WHAT DOES IT MEAN?

The first part of this petition, "do not bring us to the time of trial" or "lead us not into temptation," has been interpreted many ways, but actually no one is quite sure what Jesus meant. None of the explanations is easy to understand or to fit into our picture of God.

Perhaps the intent of this request is, "Help us to watch where we're going so we don't wander onto paths that will lead to sin." Most of us do not intend to fall into behavior that offends God's holiness, but we still find ourselves on paths that lead us there. Think of King David, Bathsheba, and her husband, Uriah, and the road they traveled because of temptation. (Read 2 Samuel 11–12 for the full story.)

David didn't have murder on his mind when he first noticed Bathsheba. He was simply relaxing, strolling on the roof of his palace when he saw her. Of course, he could have turned away from her beauty, but he didn't. He gazed a while longer. Then he sent someone to find out who she was. He could have chosen not to do that too, but he didn't. Then he had her brought to his palace. Again, he could have held back, but he didn't. In the end, David arranged for Uriah to be killed.

Week 6

The first steps down the path toward this crime did not seem horrible. After all, what's wrong with looking at a pretty woman? It's natural for a man to do so. But that is exactly the point—if we linger near the people and activities that tempt us, it will lead us to places we do not want to go, that God does not want us to go.

Another possible reading of this phrase in the Lord's Prayer makes it more active. It could mean, "Lead us away from the things that tempt us." Most of us have what I call "an arena of continuing struggle." In more old-fashioned language, this might be called our "besetting sin." It's an area where we find ourselves again and again struggling and failing. As Paul put it, "I do not do what I want, but I do the very thing I hate" (Rom. 7:15).

Reading this line of the prayer as an admission of our weaknesses acknowledges to God that we give up, that we are powerless in the face of whatever tempts us. That sense feels more like, "Get me out of here!" We are calling on God because we know our weakness, asking God to rescue us from ourselves. When we come to God this way, we say that we want the direction of our lives to change, and we want God to choose the direction. Romans 12:1-3 says, "Present your bodies as a living sacrifice. . . . Do not be conformed to this world, but be transformed by the renewing of your minds." When we invite God to direct us, we open ourselves to a new way of thinking.

No temptation that comes to us is new or unique.

THE SOURCES OF TEMPTATION

This phrase in the prayer definitely does not mean that God brings temptation into our life. James 1:13-15 says, "No one, when tempted, should say, 'I am being tempted by God'; for God cannot be tempted by evil and he himself tempts no one." Our own desire lures us. And as James continues, "When that desire has conceived, it gives birth to sin, and that sin, when fully grown, gives birth to death." The story of David and Bathsheba clearly demonstrates that reality.

So from this phrase of the prayer we take away this truth: we can and should ask God to help us pay attention to our choices and to guard our way. Being aware of the reality and strength of temptation makes us realize where some roads will lead, and we can avoid them.

Week 6

We are told to "keep alert" because our adversary, the devil, prowls about looking for "someone to devour" (1 Pet. 5:8). This phrase in the prayer guides us to seek God's help in our conflicts, to realize the consequences of our choices, and to ask for strength to resist temptation when it comes—as it inevitably will.

Christ understands our struggles. Hebrews 4:15 tells us that Jesus our high priest was in every way tempted just as we are. No temptation that comes to us is new or unique, as much as we might think otherwise. Christ knows what we face and offers us companionship as we turn from all that might lure us away from what we know is right.

THE FACE OF EVIL

Next Jesus says to pray, "Deliver us from evil." Evil has often been personified as a red creature with a goatee and pointed tail, who carries a pitchfork. We've seen this creature depicted sitting on people's shoulders, whispering to take a piece of cheesecake or buy something expensive that they don't need (not all expensive things are bad: cars, houses, appliances). In the 1970s comedian Flip Wilson built numerous routines around the catchphrase "The devil made me do it!" Making light of evil in these ways can distract us from recognizing how monstrous it is. And making evil a being allows us to place evil outside of ourselves, to make the evil in the world not about us.

Unfortunately, it is about us. Many of us would like to forget the cruelty, greed, and deceitfulness of human hearts, but we know that these often rule humans. And people like you and me, not a smoke-shrouded cartoon character, do the deeds. Greed causes executives at investment companies to raid pension funds and leave retirees destitute. Greed drives human traffickers to enslave child prostitutes around the globe and in small towns. Lust supports pornography, a multibillion dollar industry. Pride fuels the cosmetic surgery industry. Anger leads to shooting rampages like the one described in Week 5. Apathy (sloth) keeps us uninterested in doing anything about these manifestations of evil. Apathy may be the most dangerous temptation, the deadliest of the seven deadly sins, because it allows us to ignore the other six—in ourselves and in other people. Harry Emerson Fosdick's prayer (in the hymn "God of Grace and God of Glory") comes to mind: "Save us from weak resignation to the evils we deplore."

WHERE IS GOD?

Where is God in the face of the world's evil? We know that there is no place where God is not present (see Ps. 139). Though we can honestly express our feelings and pray with the psalmist and Jesus, "My God, my God, why have you forsaken me?" (Ps. 22:1; Matt. 27:46), our feelings are not a reliable gauge of God's presence or response. If we believe scripture, we know that wherever we may find ourselves, God is with us. God never leaves us to face the world's evil alone.

What we see is not the end of the story.

When we pray for God to act in the face of evil, God hears our prayers. It may seem to us that evil is winning, but what we see is not the end of the story. Theologian and teacher Walter Wink explains God's apparent silence and inaction in the face of evil by looking at the story of Daniel in Hebrew scripture. In the face of oppression from the government, Daniel prays daily for God to help him. No answer comes. On the first day that Daniel prays, God dispatches an angel with the answer. But that angel is met by an angel of darkness, and the two forces struggle, keeping the answer from reaching Daniel. Daniel is unaware of this battle going on in the spiritual realm. Wink says, "The principalities and powers are able to assert their will against the will of God, *and for a time, prevail.*" So we are to keep praying for God to "deliver us from evil." In fact, says Wink, our praying is essential for justice to come, for creation and God's creatures to be freed from oppression because "God's hands are effectively tied when we fail to pray."[2]

Writer and teacher Glenn Hinson also addressed this issue of the apparent triumph of evil:

> What are we to think about God in this interim where evil seems too often to win? . . . where we must muddle through in pain seemingly on our own? [There are] many responses to these questions. Some will say that it proves there is no God. . . . Others will go to the opposite extreme and blame God. God is the cause of everything so that whatever happens is God's will.[3]

Week 6

But humans exercise free will, and we can do things that limit God. We make choices for good and for bad, and God will not overrule us. As writer Rubem Alves has said, humans are capable of creating gardens or building concentration camps[4]—and God knows we have done both. God "*is* powerful to heal," but when individuals, businesses, and nations dump pollutants into our water, spray crops with chemicals that are known carcinogens, enslave children, torture their opponents, and brutalize entire ethnic groups, "God's ability to intervene is sometimes tragically restricted."[5]

WHY KEEP PRAYING?

If God is limited in asserting the divine will for life, why do we keep praying for evil to be obliterated? Why bother? We pray because we have hope in Christ. Christians believe that Jesus' death and resurrection dealt a mortal blow to the powers of evil. But we live in an in-between time, a time of not yet, when we are praying for God's kingdom to come while realizing that we still have a ways to go.

Christian hope is not an anemic wish for things to be different. Our hope is grounded in the goodness of God and in our trust that God will do what scripture says. This kind of grounded hope can sustain us as we pray and as we act against the world's evil.

To illustrate: When my niece was about ten, she began asking her parents for a horse. Her dad tried to discourage her by pointing out that they had no place to keep a horse. My niece suggested they could clear an area near the edge of their property for a pasture and build a small barn there. Her dad countered: that would be a lot of work. She came back with an offer to help clear the land, build the paddock, and prepare everything necessary to care for the animal. She persisted, and finally her dad agreed that if she assisted with all the work, he would assist her in buying a horse.

The two of them began immediately to create a pasture and design the barn. My niece worked harder than any of us expected a girl her age could, and after many months—more than a year— everything was ready. She got her horse (whom she named Special). She kept working steadily all those months because she trusted her

Week 6

dad. She knew he would do what he promised. Her hope and endurance were grounded in his character. That's only a faint picture of the hope Christians have, but it sheds light on what I mean by "grounded hope"—our hope grows from God's steadfast love. Because we know what God is like, because we trust that God wills good for all of us, we can keep believing that God is at work even when we don't see immediate change, even when the way is hard, even when it seems that evil triumphs.

We also keep praying because when we pray the Lord's Prayer, we become part of a network of power connecting and flowing among all believers. As we join together in praying for individuals and the world to be delivered from the grip of evil, we are doing important work that ultimately will bring down the powers of evil. To use Wink's image, whether evil is obliterated by a flash flood or by the accumulation of single drops coming one at a time, eventually the dam of oppression will be overwhelmed, and it will burst. The powers of evil will fall, overcome by the power of good.

JUST A LITTLE IS ENOUGH

Great faith is not required to pray for ourselves and the world to be delivered from evil. Jesus told us clearly that even a tiny amount of faith can move mountains—if we act on it (Matt. 17:20). We cannot accommodate ourselves to evil by saying that it is too big and we are too small. The epistle to the Romans admonishes us to "overcome evil with good" (12:21). Scripture would not include that directive if doing it were not possible.

We cannot outrun or outsmart evil, but we don't have to try. Mary's song of praise in Luke speaks of God bringing the mighty down from their thrones (1:52). God is working on delivering each one of us— every slave, every addict, every upwardly mobile professional, every crusader and reformer, every ordinary Jane and Joe—from the evil that blocks what God wants for us and for all creation.

Of course evil will not give up its throne easily. When we oppose evil with even small acts of courage, it pushes back, resisting the will of God. But knowing God is wholly good and completely faithful to the

When we oppose evil with even small acts of courage, it pushes back.

Week 6

prophets' vision, we believe that God will keep at it. Eventually the wave of our combined prayers becomes a tsunami powerful enough to sweep aside opposition to good. When we join our will and our prayers with the will of God, the kingdoms of this world will become the kingdom of our God. So we keep praying, "Deliver us from evil."

A FINAL NOTE

For thine is the kingdom, and the power,
and the glory, forever. Amen.

This phrase probably does not appear in your Bible as the conclusion of either Matthew 6 or Luke 11; most modern Bible translations include it only as a footnote if at all. Yet many of us have always said these words as the end of the prayer. People often ask why we don't have "the whole thing" when we print the Lord's Prayer in *The Upper Room* magazine. Some years ago we began quoting the prayer directly from scripture, in order not to upset readers who wanted us to quote only the version that used "trespasses" or the one that used "debts" or "sins"—whichever of those words they were accustomed to praying in worship. We have an interdenominational readership, and we did not want to seem to be favoring one tradition over another. Sticking with scripture allows us to avoid that. Since this final phrase is not in scripture, we do not include it when we print the prayer.

Where did those words come from? Scholars aren't sure. First, the phrase is called a "doxology"—a praise, as when we sing, "Praise God from whom all blessings flow." It is an ancient addition. The *Didache*, a document from the first century of the church, quotes this doxology at the end of the prayer. Some theorize that though these words were not part of the text of Matthew, a scribe copying the Bible by hand centuries later inserted this final phrase into the text. If these words of praise were a familiar addition to the prayer the scribe heard in worship, that would make sense. Perhaps a scribe thought these final words had been omitted in error and that he was setting the text right. But the oldest and most trusted manuscripts of the Gospels do not include the phrase that begins "For thine is the kingdom," and so it is not included in modern translations of the Bible. Some scholars believe the phrase is drawn from 1 Chronicles 29:11, David's blessing at the time of offerings for building the Temple:

> *Yours*, O LORD, are the greatness, *the power, the glory*, the victory, and the majesty; for all that is in the heavens and on the earth is yours; *yours is the kingdom*, O LORD, and you are exalted as head above all. . . . And now, our God, we give thanks to you and praise your glorious name.—1 Chronicles 29:11, 13, emphasis added

The italicized nouns in the doxology at the end of the Lord's Prayer are contained in the verse from First Chronicles. Perhaps this verse became linked with making offerings and was brought into corporate worship in the early church. As we know from the *Didache*, the Lord's Prayer was being used widely in Christian worship. Combining the two because they were heard close together is certainly plausible.

That series of three nouns, "the kingdom, the power, and the glory," reminds me of Jesus' three temptations in the wilderness as he prepared to begin his ministry. First, the tempter invited Jesus to turn stones into bread. This could have been a road to substantial glory. Some Gospel stories hint that the multitudes followed Jesus because he provided food. If Jesus were to meet people's physical needs by way of miracles, that would no doubt earn him fame and a huge following—a lot of glory. Then, the tempter challenged to Jesus to show off his power over natural laws by throwing himself off the Temple without being hurt. Finally, the tempter took Jesus to a mountain and offered him all the land as far as he could see—a kingdom. But Jesus resisted all three: the glory, the show of power, and the kingdom. Many of the temptations we face fall into one of those categories.

"Thine is the kingdom, and the power, and the glory" affirms that these belong not to us but to God. God is the sovereign of the universe; God is the all-powerful one; God is the one who deserves the glory. And though we are part of the larger picture of what God is doing, the future of the world does not depend on us. In Greek mythology Atlas carries the world on his shoulders. He's usually pictured bowed down by the weight of his burden. That image could just as well depict

Each of us can resign as general manager of the universe.

Week 6

many of us—carrying a heavy load of shoulds, oughts, and have-tos in the spiritual life. But these weights are not ours to carry. We don't bear the burden of doing it all. God is much bigger than anything we could ever dream up. So each of us can resign as general manager of the universe. God is God—and we are not. Reminding ourselves of that seems a wise and worthwhile way to end a time of prayer.

BACK TO THE BEGINNING

Whichever explanation you like, or whether you come up with a different one or just don't care, looking at this doxology actually takes us back neatly to where we started. The Lord's Prayer begins with recognizing God's role and praising and honoring God's holiness: "Our Father in heaven, hallowed be your name." Acknowledging God's glory is another way of doing that. "Thine is the kingdom" brings us back to "your kingdom come," to God's loving rule and will. And praying for God to supply our needs and to keep us from evil acknowledges God's power.

Jesus' outline for prayer in these passages of scripture reminds us that we are created for ongoing relationship with one another and with God. We are invited to talk with God about the small and the great matters of our days, from our daily, physical needs to the cosmic struggle between good and evil. And all along the way, as we pray and listen, God invites us to join with the rest of the family as coworkers in meeting the world's needs and reshaping the world into what God dreams it to be. Amen. Let it be so.

WEEK 6 DAILY EXAMEN

Before you get out of bed in the morning or before you fall asleep at night, look back over the preceding twenty-four hours. Then think about this:

What temptations did I face? How did God help me?

Week 6

DAILY SCRIPTURE READING AND REFLECTION

Day 1: Read James 1.

1 When was your last "trial"? Did it blindside you and emerge suddenly, or were you aware of its approach? Which of these kinds of trials affect you most?

2 How has facing struggles or failure helped you to mature? Does it always help? If so, why? If not, what conditions determine whether or not we extract good from hard times?

3 In what relationship or situation do you need wisdom right now? How can you tap into the support and guidance that God offers?

Day 2: Read 1 Corinthians 10:12-14.

1 Do you agree that there are no new temptations? Does modern culture bring us different or more difficult challenges than earlier believers faced? Which temptations are the same from century to century?

2 Think of a time when you faced temptation but were able to resist and did not give in. What "way out" did God provide? Were you aware of God's presence and guidance at the time you were being tempted?

3 What "idols" seem to capture our time, money, and attention these days? How have you recently spent a lot of time and/or money? Does that activity or relationship move you closer to being the person you feel God wants you to be?

Day 3: Read Jeremiah 17:9 and Psalm 139:23-24.

1 Is calling the heart "desperately wicked" (Jer. 17:9, KJV) or "devious above all else" and "perverse" (Jer. 17:9) too strong? How do those quotes match up with what you know of your heart? When, if ever, has your heart deceived you?

2 Why do we need God to search our heart? What is the psalmist asking for? What would you intend if you prayed this request?

3 What recent news stories cause you to agree with Jeremiah and the psalmist about the wickedness people are capable of? How do these stories move you to pray? What do you want God to do in the situations you're thinking about?

Day 4: Read Romans 7:21–8:2.

1 How have you experienced evil "close at hand"? Do you think evil exists within each of us? Why do you answer as you do?

2 Do good and evil always present themselves at the same time, as this passage suggests? When they do, what might we do to help ourselves attend to the potential for good rather than to the evil?

3 Have you experienced the internal war described here? What determines which side wins? How does Romans 8:1 apply to the preceding verses?

Day 5: Read Romans 8:34-39.

1 What comfort do you find in these verses? What do they say to you about the evil in the world?

2 Read verses 35-36 again, slowly. How do you respond to them? How do you imagine Christians in another part of the world, China or Saudi Arabia, for instance, would respond?

3 Read verses 38-39 again, slowly, pausing at each comma. Pay attention to what rises up within you. What images or feelings come to mind as you read the list? How have you experienced the truth of these verses in your life?

Preparing for the group meeting

If you have time, look back over your daily reflection pages and think about these questions:

Did you do daily examen? If so, what's your response to the practice? Did it change you or your actions?

Which of the week's scripture passages seemed particularly appropriate to something you were concerned about?

What in this week's readings most challenged or surprised you?

Meeting Notes/Responses

LEADER'S GUIDE

This guide offers plans for leading a study group through six weekly meetings. Each session includes these components:

Opening Prayer and Music
Discussion of Daily Reflections
Going Deeper (group activity)
Lectio Divina (if you meet for 90 minutes)
Closing Prayer and Music

At the end of each session's directions, you'll find a "looking ahead" list. This outlines how to prepare for the next week's meeting.

ADVANCE PUBLICITY

Generally, people remember an item of information after hearing it five times. About six weeks before the first group meeting, begin to publicize the upcoming Lord's Prayer study group. Promote it in your church newsletter and on bulletin boards; on the church Web site and in the Sunday bulletins; and with announcements during worship, adult church-school classes, and other gatherings.

BEFORE THE FIRST MEETING

The small-group meeting is meant to occur at the end of each week. If you intend participants to read the first chapter and complete the daily scripture readings before the first meeting, order books in time to receive and distribute them about two weeks in advance. You may want to send postcards or e-mail messages to group members reminding them to read the first chapter and accompanying daily scripture readings to prepare for the first meeting.

Another option is to hold a short introductory meeting a week or two before the first session. Plan on about forty-five minutes. Use this time not only to introduce the study and distribute books but also to invite group members to get acquainted and begin praying for one another, for the group leader(s), and for the study.

YOUR MAIN TASK

Your main task as leader will be establishing a welcoming atmosphere. For most people, prayer is a deeply personal subject. The material for Week 1 recognizes that many of us feel inadequate when it comes to praying on our own and establishing a regular practice. This is especially true of praying aloud in public, so if you want group members to do this, ask ahead of time. This will give people the opportunity to prepare themselves or to decline privately. Unless you know that someone prays comfortably in public, do not ask anyone directly to pray during a session. Asking for a volunteer to pray is less stressful.

Group members probably will need encouragement and an honest example from you in talking about your struggles and shortcomings in prayer in order to talk freely about theirs. Model this in your responses to activities. An honest, open atmosphere will free participants to explore what God may be saying to them during these weeks through scripture and through interaction within the group.

WEEKLY SESSIONS

Whenever possible, distribute supplies and handouts before people arrive in order to limit disruption during the group time.

Participants will be invited to spend time in each session reviewing their responses to that week's daily scripture readings and then talking about them with one or two other group members. State clearly that anyone can choose at any time not to respond to a question during discussions—whether questions are posed in the study or asked by another group member. All they need to say is "pass"; discussion will move to the next person, without pressure or comment.

MUSIC

Many musical settings of the Lord's Prayer are available; some may be familiar to the group already. Several can be found in *The Upper Room Worshipbook*. Consider singing or listening to a few during the first session. You could play this music as the group gathers. Make music an ongoing feature of your meetings: choose a different musical setting of the Lord's Prayer each week, use the same version every week for continuity, or use the same version to begin each meeting and vary the version used at closing. Even if using music is a stretch for you, remember that for some group members, the listening or singing may be the most meaningful or memorable part of the study.

A NEW WAY TO LISTEN TO SCRIPTURE: *LECTIO DIVINA*

Lectio divina is an ancient way of listening for God's guidance through scripture. Teaching group members to approach scripture in this way will offer them a tool that can help them learn to recognize God's voice and receive personal guidance from their time with scripture.

If you are familiar with leading this form of scripture reflection, what follows will be a review. If this is a new process for you, these instructions will be sufficient to guide you in leading the process. Trust the process. It will work. Some group members may find that they have been reading scripture in this way for years; they've simply not known the "official" term for what they do (and they don't need to).

Because leading a group through the process takes about forty-five minutes, a longer session (ninety minutes) is required for *lectio*.

Lectio divina is a Latin phrase that means "sacred reading" or "holy reading." You may or may not introduce the Latin term to the group. Use your own judgment. *Lectio divina* as you will lead it during this study has the following steps, each concluded with a period of silence for individual reflection:

- hearing the scripture read aloud (several times)
- reflecting on a word or phrase from the passage
- connecting the word or phrase to individual situations
- listening for an invitation from God in the passage
- praying for God's help to respond to the invitation

Introducing *Lectio Divina*

If you include *lectio*, group reflection on scripture, in each session, you will need to introduce this way of listening to scripture to the group in the first session. This approach differs—perhaps markedly—from the way Bible study groups usually approach scripture. Traditional Bible study methods grow from an educational model that most of us learned in school. We approach written material to read it, outline it, analyze it, look for patterns, compare and contrast it with other material, finish it, close the book. Typically we carry this model into reading scripture—but the Bible is not like other books.

Hebrews 4:12 says that the Word of God is "living and active"; the living message of God has something new to say to us every day. No matter how familiar a passage may be, if we approach with a listening heart, God can use it to speak a new word of guidance, comfort, and challenge to us. Dietrich Bonhoeffer wrote in *Life Together* that believers approach scripture "on the strength of the promise that it has something utterly personal to say to us for this day and for our Christian life."[1] Participating in *lectio divina* in the group will help people learn how to listen for God's personal word to them whenever they read the Bible.

Though this method is simple, it is not always easy. Because our education trains us to analyze and dissect, when we hear a Bible passage being read, it is often difficult just to listen to the actual words. For example, we ask group members to listen to the story of the widow who refused to give up and kept asking a judge for help (Luke 18:1-8). We say (as you will in leading *lectio divina*), "Listen for a word or phrase that stops you, that gets your attention, that stands out for you." Then we invite group members to repeat "their" word or phrase. Someone may say "perseverance" or "determination"; neither of those words appears in the Bible passage. A hearer who responds in this way is saying something *about* what was read.

Describing the passage or commenting on situations mentioned in it shows that we have stepped back from the actual words. We read a passage and declare that it is about compassion or faith or doubt or something else. Or we read it looking for "the lesson." We compare a passage to other Bible passages; we analyze; we define words.

Lectio divina guides us to another approach—allowing the text to shape to us. The goal of *lectio divina* is not mastering the text but permitting the text to master us, to form us.[2] We read the Bible not to get to the end of it (as we do a novel or a textbook) but to get to what is, for us, the heart of it for this day, in our situation. The analytical, educational approach is so deeply ingrained in us that you may need more than once to guide the group members gently back to the actual words of the passage. Some people will need a few weeks' practice to be able to listen this way without reminders. Emphasize that they will be hearing—not reading—the passage. Tell them specifically not to read along in their own Bibles. (The different translations that would inevitably be used will set off comparison/contrast thinking about why the words are different and pondering why we need different translations and so on, all examples of thinking about rather than listening to the passage.)

You may use photocopies of the next two pages as handouts as you explain *lectio divina* in your group. If you prefer, write the content on newsprint or whiteboard as you lead the exploration of scripture.

OBSTACLES TO HEARING GOD IN SCRIPTURE

COMMON OBSTACLES

- thinking/talking about scripture
- classifying
- comparing
- describing
- explaining
- looking for "the lesson" rather than listening to scripture:

  > the actual words that are there
  >
  > the emotions we feel
  >
  > the connections we make
  >
  > the memories that arise

INFORMATIONAL AND FORMATIONAL READING

Reading for information is an integral part of teaching and learning. But reading is also concerned with listening for the special guidance, for the particular insight that enhances your relationship with God. What matters is the attitude of mind and heart.

INFORMATIONAL READING

1. Informational reading is concerned with covering as much material as possible and as quickly as possible.
2. Informational reading is linear—|seeking an objective meaning, truth, or principle to apply.
3. Informational reading seeks to master the text.
4. In informational reading, the text is an object out there for us to control.
5. Informational reading is analytical, critical, and judgmental.
6. Informational reading is concerned with problem solving.

FORMATIONAL READING

1. Formational reading is concerned with small portions of content rather than quantity.
2. Formational reading focuses on depth and seeks multiple layers of meaning in a single passage.
3. Formational reading allows the text to master the student.
4. Formational reading sees the student as the object to be shaped by the text.
5. Formational reading requires a humble, detached, willing, loving approach.
6. Formational reading is open to mystery. Students come to the scripture to stand before the Mystery called God and to let the Mystery address them.

Adapted from information in *Shaped by the Word: The Power of Scripture in Spiritual Formation,* rev. ed., by M. Robert Mulholland Jr. (Nashville, TN: Upper Room Books, 2000), 49–63. Used by permission of Upper Room Books.

GUIDING A GROUP THROUGH *LECTIO DIVINA*

Before you begin

- Recruit someone from the group to read the scripture passage on the third round. Provide a Bible with the passage marked or make a photocopy of it. (Enlarged print is helpful for many readers.)
- Divide the larger group into groups of three or four and have them move into seating arrangements for conversation.

Do not attempt this process with more than four people in the groups; you will not have time to complete the process in the time allotted. Invite people to bring this book and/or their journal with them into the smaller groups.

STEP 1: Invite the group members to get comfortable. Tell them what is going to happen: They will hear a scripture passage being read four times, once by an alternate reader, with silence and then group time after each hearing. After each reading, you will invite them to reflect in silence. When you end the silent reflection, you will guide them through the next step of the process.

STEP 2: Tell participants what passage you will be reading. Ask them to listen for a word or phrase that stops them, gets their attention, evokes an emotional response. Read the selected passage through twice, more slowly the second time.

STEP 3: After the reading, invite people to reflect in silence on "their" word or phrase. Allow one minute of silence. (Time it so you do not shortchange the process.)

STEP 4: Invite people to repeat in their groups without additional comment their word or phrase. (The "without additional comment" is nearly impossible for people to do.) Have them begin with the person seated nearest you.

STEP 5: Read the passage again, asking people to listen to hear how this passage connects to their life right now.

STEP 6: After the reading, remind them to think in silence about how the passage connects to their life today. Invite them to be open to a song, a sensory impression, a color—anything that arises for them. Allow two minutes of silence.

STEP 7: Invite people to say a few sentences in their group about the connection they sensed. Have them begin with the person seated farthest from you.

STEP 8: Have the alternate reader read the passage this time. Ask the group members to listen this time for an invitation from God for their life in the next twenty-four to forty-eight hours—not the rest of their life; just the next day or two.

STEP 9: Invite the group members to reflect in silence on the invitation they hear. Allow three minutes of silence.

STEP 10: Invite conversation in small groups. Ask people to talk about the invitation they sense from God for their lives in the next few days. Have them begin with the person to the left of whoever began last time.

STEP 11: Invite the people to pray for one another in their small groups, asking God to empower each one to respond to the invitation s/he heard. They may pray silently or aloud. Ask everyone to remain silent after their group finishes praying, until everyone is silent. End your time of *lectio divina* by saying amen before moving on.

SUMMARY OF *LECTIO*

1. Invite hearers to listen for a word or phrase that gets their attention. Read the selected passage through twice, more slowly the second time. Invite them to reflect in silence on "their" word or phrase.

2. After one minute of silence, invite people to repeat in their groups without additional comment their word or phrase.

3. Read the passage again, asking people to listen to hear how this passage connects to their life right now. Invite silence to reflect. (Two minutes.)

4. After two minutes of silence, invite people to say a few sentences each in their group about the connection they sensed.

5. Alternate reader reads the passage. Ask group members to listen this time for an invitation from God for their life in the next day or two. Invite silence. (Three minutes.)

6. After three minutes of silence, ask people to talk in their groups about the invitation they heard.

7. Invite the people to pray for one another one by one, asking God to empower each one to respond to the invitation s/he heard.

DAILY EXAMEN

The *examen* is an ancient spiritual practice linked most closely to Ignatius of Loyola. Ignatius created a series of "spiritual exercises" that led users into deep reflection (and took thirty days in retreat to complete). But examen can also be a single question used for reflection on arising or at bedtime. Using a single question over a long period enables us to focus on a central issue in the spiritual journey.

The daily examen cultivates mindfulness of God in the midst of daily activities. Encourage group members not to think of the questions as another task on a to-do list but as a way to help them pay attention. You may display the coming week's question on newsprint or whiteboard in each meeting.

MATERIALS AND SUPPLIES

For every session: Bibles, name tags, newsprint or whiteboard and markers, music for group singing, perhaps a bell (with a pleasant tone) to mark time and call participants together after activities.

A list of additional supplies needed for each session appears at the end of the preceding week's session.

PREPARING FOR SESSION 1

- Read the chapter, noting passages that evoke response.
- Complete the daily scripture readings and reflection.
- Arrange for music.
- Write psalm references (see list below) on strips of paper for the Going Deeper activity.
- Photocopy the handout(s) about *lectio divina* if it will be part of your sessions and recruit someone to be the second reader.

- Prepare to lead *lectio* by reading the directions until you are comfortable with the process. Mark in the Bible or photocopy the scripture passage for the alternate reader.
- Prepare a simple focal point for opening and closing, such as a white Christ candle and objects fitting for the season of the year. Remember to bring matches or a candlelighter.
- Copy the key words of the sample group covenant onto newsprint or a whiteboard before the meeting (see page 9).

WEEK 1 GROUP SESSION

This session differs slightly from subsequent weeks because it includes explanation of the study's overall format. You will establish a group covenant about confidentiality. Expect the session to run as long as an hour and forty-five minutes unless you have a separate introductory meeting (see pages 113–114). *Approximate* times given here will help you structure the meeting.

OPENING PRAYER AND MUSIC (5 MINUTES)

Light the Christ candle, saying, *Christ is present wherever two or three believers gather.* Pray this prayer:

Loving God, thank you for each of these people who want to know you more deeply and serve you more faithfully. Thank you for this time you have given us to learn from you and from one another. Teach us to pray and to live so that those who know us will see your kingdom being made real in our lives. Amen.

If you are not comfortable leading group singing, use recorded music or recruit an assistant from within the group. Suggested chorus: "I Want to Know You More."

INTRODUCING ONE ANOTHER (10 MINUTES)

Invite group members to pair up with someone they don't know or don't know well. Ask them to answer the questions below. Read each question and pause for ten seconds of silence after each one, before conversation begins. Allow one minute per person for each response:

1. How did you come to have the name that you have?
2. What is your earliest memory about prayer?
3. What do you hope to get out of this study? Why are you here?

If group members do not know one another well, invite people to introduce their partners to the entire group in thirty seconds or less.

INTRODUCING THE STUDY (5–8 MINUTES)

Invite group members to look at page 7 in the Introduction. Point out these features of each week's material:

Short chapter to read to begin each week
Suggested daily scripture readings and written responses
Small-group meeting

Ask for a show of hands of those who keep or have kept a spiritual journal. Request comments on what people gain from this practice. If you have kept a journal, model a response by commenting briefly about your experience. By writing responses in the space this book provides each week, participants have a chance to try journaling.

DAILY EXAMEN (2 MINUTES)

Point out the questions provided at the end of each week and mention using them in early morning on waking or at night before rest.

ESTABLISH A GROUP COVENANT (5 MINUTES)

Review the list from page 9 and ask for suggested additions.

DISCUSSION OF DAILY REFLECTIONS (10 MINUTES)

Invite group members to sit in pairs with someone they don't know or don't know well. If group members did not have their books ahead of time, invite them to look at the suggested scripture and reflection questions for Day 3 of Week 1. Allow five minutes for them to read the scripture passage and write answers to the first two questions for that day. Then ask them to comment to each other about their responses to the questions. Allow two minutes per person for discussion.

Ask participants to form groups of three and look at Preparing for the Group Meeting section at the end of Week 1 (page 30). Allow one minute per person to comment about something that challenged them or to say which scripture applied to a personal situation.

GOING DEEPER (15 MINUTES)

This exercise explores images of God in the Psalms. Allow each person to select a strip of paper with a reference to a psalm. Look at as many passages as you have people in the group. (To be sure that passages representing varied images are reviewed, put references into the container in numerical order—#1 first, then #2, and so on until there are as many slips of paper as there are people in the group.)

1. Psalm 23:1-3	7. Psalm 139:1-12
2. Psalm 24:7-10	8. Psalm 146:5-10
3. Psalm 18:1-3	9. Psalm 64:7-9
4. Psalm 96:10-13	10. Psalm 136:1-9, 23-26
5. Psalm 103:8-14	11. Psalm 27:1-3
6. Psalm 135:5-12	12. Psalm 62:5-8

Ask group members to spend seven minutes in silence reading the verses and thinking about the picture of God presented in them, reflecting on these questions:

What does this passage say directly to you about God's nature?

What does it suggest indirectly about God?

What does it suggest to you about human nature?

Ring the bell to call the group back together and ask them to name attributes of God they saw in the passages they read. List these attributes down the left side of a newsprint sheet or whiteboard. Leave the right side blank. Remind or tell them of Dr. Lieber's comment that Jewish people have been heavily influenced by the book of Psalms in their worship and prayer.

At the top on the right side of the newsprint/board, write "Our Father." Ask group members to look at the list on the left and consider how God as a father is like or not like each item on it. After you've gone down the list, spend a minute in silence. Then ask, "How does Jesus' suggesting that we call God 'father' invite us into a different relationship than we see in these psalms?" Point out the greater warmth, mutuality, and responsiveness in the image of God as father compared to God as rock, king, avenger, even shepherd (sheep are very dumb, are animals and therefore mute).

Finally, pose this question: *What does this reflection say to you about our praying "Our Father in heaven"?*

LECTIO DIVINA (45 MINUTES)

Use John 1:35-39*a* (end with "Come and see.") Distribute the handout "Informational and Formational Reading." Spend a few minutes talking about the content. Point out that this way of approaching scripture probably differs from their usual practice. Preview the steps of the process, emphasizing that each step will be followed by silence and that you will direct them step by step. You may want to display the five underlined words from this list along with the reference for the passage you will be using.

- *hearing* the scripture read aloud (several times)
- *reflecting* on a word or phrase from the passage
- *connecting* the word or phrase to individual's situations
- *listening* for an invitation from God in the passage
- *praying* for God's help to respond to the invitation

Remember to have everyone move into small groups before you begin. For this session, have no more than three persons per group, since the explanation will take up part of the forty-five minutes. Use the *lectio divina* process outlined on pages 120–121. Once you become accustomed to the process, you may use the summary (page 121).

CLOSING PRAYER AND MUSIC (5 MINUTES)

Point out the examen question(s) suggested for the coming week displayed in the room (on whiteboard or newsprint).

Preparation for prayer: Invite group members to name people who have taught them something about prayer and to speak one sentence about what they learned from the person. Then invite people to name persons and situations they'd like group members to pray for in the coming week. End the time of prayer by singing or listening to the Lord's Prayer. Then pray this closing prayer or one of your own:

O God, thank you for the gift of prayer and for inviting us into relationship with you. We hold in the light of your love the people and situations we've just named. (Silence) Now help us to put legs on our prayers during this week. Amen.

PREPARING FOR SESSION 2

- Read the chapter, noting passages you respond to.
- Complete the daily scripture readings and reflection.
- Create signs with names of Bible characters for the Going Deeper exploration (see list in session content).
- Review directions for leading *lectio divina* if you are new to guiding groups through the process.
- Mark or photocopy the scripture passage for *lectio divina* for the alternate reader.
- Photocopy the handout "The Breath Prayer."

WEEK 2 GROUP SESSION

OPENING PRAYER AND MUSIC (5 MINUTES)

Invite group members to stand in a circle. Begin by listening to or singing the Lord's Prayer. Then light the Christ candle, saying,

> *Come, Creator of light; illumine us.*
> *Come, incarnate Light, and fill us.*
> *Come, Holy Spirit, fire of God, and set us aflame.*

Ask people to reflect for a moment on how they usually address God—the name they use for God—when they pray on their own, and why the address holds meaning for them. After a minute of silence, invite comments. Follow with this prayer or one of your own:

O God, we give thanks that you come to us no matter what name we use to call on you. We give thanks that you come to us even when we do not remember to call. And we give thanks that you are here with us now. Help each of us to hear your message in our words to one another. Amen.

THE BREATH PRAYER

"Pray without ceasing," the Bible tells us (1 Thess. 5:17). How could anyone ever do that? Centuries ago, a Russian peasant decided to try to find a way. He walked across Eastern Europe, searching for continual connection with God. The story of his journey is told in the Christian devotional classic *The Way of a Pilgrim*.

As he walked, he began reciting a prayer familiar to most Christians, "Lord Jesus Christ, Son of God, have mercy on me, a sinner" with the rhythm of his breathing. As he inhaled, he said, "Lord Jesus Christ, Son of God"; as he exhaled, he said, "Have mercy on me, a sinner." Because this prayer was joined with the rhythm of breathing, it became known as the "breath prayer."

Some people shortened the prayer, opening with, "Lord Jesus Christ" and ending with, "Have mercy on me." Over time it was shortened even more, to simply, "Jesus" and "have mercy." This extremely shortened form came to be called the Jesus Prayer. Calling on God as we breathe in signifies welcoming God; asking God for help while breathing out signifies letting go of all that is not God and what God wants for us.

In recent times, Christians have adapted this idea of a continual prayer to create modern breath prayers. These breath prayers consist of an address to God and a petition that reflects a current concern. Each part of the prayer has six to eight syllables. We might pray, "God of love, fill me with love" (or, "Fill me with peace," or ". . . with joy"). We pray this very short personal prayer as often as possible throughout each day. For example, we can pray a personal breath prayer while we wait for a phone to be answered, a computer to boot up, a checkout line to move, a traffic light to change. Or we can connect the prayer to common actions: opening a door, starting the car, saving work on the computer. These actions become reminders to pray the prayer and turn our thoughts to God.

Personal breath prayers change over time to reflect changing concerns.

DISCUSSION OF DAILY REFLECTIONS (10 MINUTES)

Direct people to Preparing for Your Group Meeting at the end of Week 2. Allow two minutes of silence for review and reflection before discussion. Give two minutes per person to comment about what in the week's readings evoked a response in them. Then invite discussion of these questions for the remaining two minutes: *Does God have a specific will for each of us on each day of our lives? If so, how do we discover what it is? If not, what does "doing God's will" mean?*

GOING DEEPER (20 MINUTES)

This activity will lead to introduction of the breath prayer. First, the group explores Mark 10:46-52. Create signs with names of the characters in this story in large letters: Jesus, Bartimaeus (a man who was blind), the disciples, crowd members who tell Bartimaeus to be quiet, crowd members who help him get to Jesus. Post or place the signs around the room where they can be seen. After reading the story aloud, invite people to stand near the character they most identify with. (Not all the roles may be taken; don't worry about that and tell the group not to worry about it either.) Once group members choose a character, ask them to discuss with the others who join them:

Why do I identify with this character?
What was God's will for my character in this situation?
How did the others support or block God's will being done for or through my character?

After five minutes, take five minutes to let groups summarize their conversation for the full group. (Adjust time depending on number of small groups.) Ask how we—as individuals and the church—listen to or silence those in need around us.

Together look at the handout about the breath prayer. Point out the prayer in the second paragraph and explain that you will lead the group through it. You will say the words aloud several times while group members pray them silently. Then you will stop praying aloud while they continue silently praying until you say amen.

Say the prayer aloud for one minute. Allow them another minute.

After the silence, direct attention again to the handout, to the section about personal breath prayers. Invite people first to think about what they would want or need to call God right now—"God of all comfort," "heavenly Father," "O God, my light," other. Then ask them to think about what they would ask Jesus to do for them and form a short petition—six or eight syllables in length. They won't tell anyone their prayers. Invite them to pray their individual breath prayers, explaining you will say amen to conclude the time. Allow two minutes.

Suggest that group members pray their breath prayers as often as possible during the coming week as a way to pray "without ceasing."

LECTIO DIVINA (45 MINUTES)

The passage for this week is Matthew 22:17-21. After the time of reflection and prayer, invite group members to note in their book anything they want to remember from the time with scripture.

CLOSING PRAYER AND MUSIC (5 MINUTES)

Point out the examen questions for the coming week. Listen to or sing a setting of the Lord's Prayer. Invite group members to name news items that show God's will either clearly being done or clearly not being done, then guide a closing prayer with the following sentences, allowing silence after each.

Loving God, we ask your wisdom for all who lead. (Silence)

Compassionate God, we ask that your will be done for the weak, the vulnerable, those who have no one to speak for them. (Silence)

Healing God, we ask wholeness for those who are ill, and help for those who need medical care but don't have it. (Silence)

Provider God, feed those who hunger for bread, for meaning, for hope. (Silence)

Liberating God, give freedom to those held captive by their own and others' desires. (Silence)

Peace-loving God, bring your peace to those whose lives are disrupted by war and violence. (Silence)

Sheltering God, we pray for ourselves:

> *For our state, our town, our neighbors.* (Silence)

> *For this congregation.* (Silence)

For each household and family represented here. (Silence)
For each one of us. (Silence)
Grant us ears to hear your call and courage to live according to
your will. Amen.

PREPARING FOR SESSION 3

- Read the chapter, noting passages you respond to.
- Complete the daily scripture readings and reflection.
- Using magazines, art books, and other available sources, collect images (photographs, drawings, paintings) to use in the
  Going Deeper activity. Look for pictures of individuals and
  groups engaged in various activities. Try to get an assortment
  representing urban, suburban, and rural settings; different
  ethnic and socioeconomic groups; home, business, school settings; indoor and outdoor activities, etc. Make copies of the
  handout "Praying with Pictures" (page 134).
- Recruit someone to be the second reader if you will be including *lectio divina*. Mark in the Bible or photocopy the *lectio*
  scripture passage for the reader. Review directions for leading
  lectio divina.
- If possible, arrange to bake bread or cookies in the meeting
  area so the aroma is present when group members arrive.
  (A countertop oven can be used to bake several cookies or
  biscuits at a time.) Of course, encourage people to eat the
  cookies or biscuits (bring butter, jelly, and knives if you bake
  biscuits) as you gather. You may invite a group member who
  enjoys cooking or baking to arrange this setup.

WEEK 3 GROUP SESSION

OPENING PRAYER AND MUSIC (5 MINUTES)

Begin by inviting group members to enjoy the cookies or biscuits if
you have them as they gather. Listen to or sing the Lord's Prayer. Light
the Christ candle and remind the group that in doing so we welcome
Christ into our conversation and reflection. Invite group members to

name ways God has fed them since the last meeting. Invite them to name ways they have fed others.

After all who wish to have spoken, pray this prayer or your own:

Bread of heaven, feed us during this time together that we may be strengthened to offer your love to all we meet. Amen.

DISCUSSION OF DAILY REFLECTIONS (10 MINUTES)

Direct people to Preparing for Your Group Meeting at the end of Week 3. Allow two minutes of silence for review and reflection before discussion. Give two minutes per person to comment about what in the week's readings evoked a response in them. Then invite them to discuss this question for remaining two minutes: *What responsibility do churches and individual Christians have in eliminating hunger and poverty in the world?*

GOING DEEPER (20 MINUTES)

In this exercise, participants will pray with pictures.[3] See suggestions about types of pictures to provide in the weekly supply list above. Place pictures face down on a table. Invite each person to select a picture at random, without looking at it. Distribute the handout "Praying with Pictures" (page 134), and direct participants to write responses on the sheet. After ten minutes, have group members pair up to talk about what they experienced. After three minutes of conversation, invite comments and insights.

LECTIO DIVINA (45 MINUTES)

This week's passage is Luke 12:27-30. After the time of reflection and prayer, invite group members to note in their book anything they want to remember from the time with scripture.

CLOSING PRAYER AND MUSIC (5 MINUTES)

Point out the examen questions for the coming week. Listen to or sing the Lord's Prayer. Invite group members to name three gifts God has given: a person who makes a difference in their daily life, an object that has special meaning for them, and an intangible treasure.

Close with this prayer or one of your own:

For all your good gifts, we give you thanks, O Lord. Show us how we can embody your gracious provision in the lives of those we encounter this week. Amen.

PREPARING FOR SESSION 4

- Read the chapter, noting passages you respond to.
- Complete the daily scripture readings and reflection.
- Assemble supplies for Going Deeper activity: a pitcher filled with water, a large bowl, and towels; paper that dissolves in water *or* water-soluble pencils (the writing washes off a piece of paper when it is placed in water). Check arts and crafts stores, education supply houses, or online for these products.
- Recruit someone to be the second reader if you will be including *lectio divina* and mark in the Bible or photocopy the *lectio* scripture passage for the reader. Review the directions for leading *lectio*.
- Meditative music and a player

WEEK 4 GROUP SESSION

OPENING PRAYER (5 MINUTES)

Light the Christ candle as a sign of Christ's presence.

Begin by listening to or singing the Lord's Prayer (or both). Then invite group members to spend time praying their breath prayers, letting them know you will end the prayer time by saying amen. After two minutes, say amen. Ask if anyone has comments about using the breath prayer. Conclude with this prayer or one of your own:

O God, you are closer to us than our breath. May we live in daily awareness of your nearness. We welcome you to our time together in this session. Amen.

PRAYING WITH PICTURES

Choose a picture and take time to look at it carefully. Use the questions below to guide further reflection. Don't feel that you must answer all or any of them; these are suggestions. Write your responses, and then write a prayer.

What do you see, feel, and hear? What is the human story behind the picture?

What passage or passages of scripture come to mind, and what is the connection between them and the picture?

What does God see, hear, feel, and want to do? Write a conversation with God (you write both parts) about what the picture represents to you. (Use back of sheet to continue.)

What is Christ saying to me through my response to the photo?

My prayer:

DISCUSSION OF DAILY REFLECTIONS (10 MINUTES)

Direct people to Preparing for Your Group Meeting at the end of Week 4. Allow two minutes of silence for review and reflection before discussion. Give two minutes per person for comments on responses evoked by the week's readings. In the remaining two minutes invite participants to discuss: *What is your definition of sin?*

GOING DEEPER (20 MINUTES)

Arrange the bowl and pitcher of water on a central table or somewhere else in the room where all can see it. Ask for a volunteer to read aloud Romans 3:21-26. Distribute either the pencils that produce washable markings or the paper that dissolves in water. Invite group members to find a place where they can write privately. Play meditative music during this reflection time. Using the special paper or the special pencils, each person is invited to write phrases that represent acts or attitudes for which they want to ask forgiveness. (Assure them that no one will see what they write.) After several minutes, call the group back. Read or say these words from 1 John 1:9:

If we confess our sins, he who is faithful and just will forgive us our sins and cleanse us from all unrighteousness.

Pour water from the pitcher into the bowl and invite group members to come forward with their requests for forgiveness. Depending on the materials being used, they will either dissolve their paper in the water or dissolve the writing on the sheet by moving it through the water. If the latter, let individuals blot the paper on a towel and take the empty sheet as a reminder of God's forgiveness. After everyone who wishes to has come to the bowl of water, invite the group to sing a chorus about forgiveness such as "Change My Heart, O God." Now invite people to say to one another, "In the name of Jesus Christ, you are forgiven."

LECTIO DIVINA (45 MINUTES)

This week's passage is Luke 22:31-34. After the time of reflection and prayer, invite group members to note in their book anything they want to remember from the time with scripture.

CLOSING PRAYER AND MUSIC (5 MINUTES)

Direct group members to the examen question(s) for the coming week. Listen to or sing the Lord's Prayer. Invite group members to reflect in silence on this question: *What does being forgiven feel like?* After two minutes of silence, invite people to say a single word that describes the feelings they associate with being forgiven. End by praying this prayer or one of your own:

Forgiving God, thank you for your patience with us. Thank you for forgiving us day by day. Amen.

PREPARING FOR SESSION 5

- Read the chapter, noting passages you respond to.
- Complete the daily scripture readings and reflection.
- Recruit someone to be the second reader if you will be including *lectio divina* and mark in the Bible or photocopy the *lectio* scripture for the reader. Review directions for leading *lectio*.
- Photocopy the handout for Going Deeper activity, "Debtors' Prison Reflection."
- Blank paper and colored pencils
- Loose keys, one per person; a basket

WEEK 5 GROUP SESSION

OPENING PRAYER AND MUSIC (5 MINUTES)

Light the Christ candle. Begin by listening to or singing the Lord's Prayer. Invite group members to reflect in silence on this question: *Where in the past week have I seen evidence of forgiveness?* After a minute of silence, ask group members to describe the images of forgiveness they have seen. Then pray this prayer or one of your own:

Holy God, we know that we are not holy. But by your grace, we have been forgiven. Help us, each one of us, to know ourselves as your beloved child, fully welcomed into relationship with you. In this time together, open our eyes to see and our hearts to feel the fullness of forgiveness that you offer us over and over again. In the name of the Christ, Jesus, we pray. Amen.

Debtors' Prison Reflection

1. Have you ever been held in someone's "debtors' prison"? If so, what put you there, and how did it feel to be unforgiven? If not, what do you imagine it would feel like?

2. Who has been or was in your debtors' prison? If you have freed the person(s) there, how did that come about? If you currently are holding people in your prison, what will it take for you to release them?

3. How long do you keep people in your debtors' prison? Do you see any patterns in why or how you place them there and what it takes for you to be willing to release them?

4. What offenses cause you to put someone in your debtors' prison? Have you ever felt inclined to brand groups of people guilty forever? How do you think God feels about these people? What does God want for them?

Based on Matthew 18:21-33   *© by Upper Room Books*
Permission is granted to make one copy for each participant.
The Lord's Prayer Session 5 Handout

DISCUSSION OF DAILY REFLECTIONS (10 MINUTES)

After forming groups of three, direct people to Preparing for Your Group Meeting at the end of Week 5. Allow two minutes of silence for review and reflection before discussion. Give two minutes per person for comments on responses evoked by the week's readings. In the remaining two minutes invite participants to discuss: *What does being forgiven feel like?*

GOING DEEPER (20 MINUTES)

This scripture-exploration exercise is based on the parable of the unforgiving servant in Matthew 18:21-33. Group members will be given time alone to complete "Debtors' Prison Reflection." To begin, distribute blank paper and colored pencils. Direct group members to draw or write something that represents feelings they hear described in the parable you are about to read. Read Matthew 18:21-33 aloud. Read it again, more slowly.

Next, distribute the handout "Debtors' Prison Reflection." Group members are to find a place where they can spend a few minutes alone, prayerfully reflecting on the parable in response to the questions on the worksheet.

After ten minutes, call the group together. Place the assorted keys on a table or in a basket to pass around. Invite individuals to take a key as a reminder to unlock their personal debtors' prison every day. Or, if they are unwilling to unlock it, suggest they take a key as a sign of intention to allow God to move them toward forgiving. Then people may signal their intention by tearing up the debtors' prison worksheet, discarding it into a container so you can carry the offenses away. (If a metal trash can or grill is available, you might burn the pieces, but only if you won't set off a fire alarm or sprinkler system.)

LECTIO DIVINA (45 MINUTES)

This week's passage is Colossians 3:12-15. After the time of reflection and prayer, invite group members to note in their book anything they want to remember from the time with scripture.

Closing Prayer and Music (5 minutes)

Point out the examen question(s) for the coming week. Sing or listen to the Lord's Prayer. Ask group members to reflect in silence on how they might dismantle their personal "debtors' prison." Invite sentence prayers to be spoken aloud. Close the session with this prayer or one of your own:

> *Forgiving God, you have set us free. Help us to do the same for those we have held in our debtors' prisons. Show us the path that will lead us to forgive fully. In the name of Christ we pray. Amen.*

Preparing for Session 6

- Read the chapter, noting passages you respond to.
- Complete the daily scripture readings and reflection.
- Prepare small slips of paper for opening prayer. (Bring pens and pencils too.)
- Find a bowl or other container to use during opening and closing prayer.
- Recruit someone to be the second reader if you will be including *lectio divina* and mark in the Bible or photocopy the *lectio* scripture passage for the reader. Review directions for leading *lectio.*

Week 6 Group Session

Opening Prayer and Music (5 minutes)

Listen to or sing the Lord's Prayer. Light the Christ candle. Distribute two small pieces of paper and pen or pencil to each group member. Ask everyone to think back over the weeks of the study and identify one new idea about prayer and one idea or practice that may make praying easier for them. Once people have these in mind, have them write each idea on a slip of paper and fold those slips. Invite group members to stand in a circle. Pass a bowl to collect the papers and place them near the Christ candle. Light the candle and pray this prayer or one of your own:

Holy God, we marvel that you reach out to us. We thank you for prayer, the gift that builds a bridge between you and us. Thank you for your steadfast love that bears with us in our sin and moves us toward what you want for us. In this time together, enable us to hear your message in the words we say to one another. Amen.

DISCUSSION OF DAILY REFLECTIONS (10 MINUTES)

Direct people to Preparing for Your Group Meeting at the end of Week 6. Give them two minutes each to comment on responses evoked by the week's readings. Then in the remaining time, invite discussion of this question: *What does being forgiven feel like?*

GOING DEEPER (20 MINUTES)

In this exercise participants will experience letting go of responsibility for the universe by releasing concerns into God's loving care. Tell them that people respond differently to this process and that whatever they experience is fine. *Read or summarize this introduction:*

Most of us have little experience with silence or inactivity. How many of us haven't been on a silent retreat because it sounds impossible or torturous? How many of us are rarely at home without a television, radio, stereo, or iPod playing? How many of us never turn off our cell phones except in church, and sometimes not even then? We live frenetically, as if everything depends on staying busy and completing our to-do list. Even in serving God we continually strive, as if we personally must do all that needs to be done. This is a lie. God was at work before we came along, and God will still be at work when we are long gone. Transforming the world is God's work; we are short-term participants in the process. We can be more obedient participants than we sometimes are, but the overall agenda is God's, not ours.

To begin the exercise, say:

We are going to experiment with deepening silence, releasing our cares in God's presence, using Psalm 46:10. Most of the time we will be silent. We can do this. I will guide you through the process by repeating parts of the verse and inviting you to reflect in silence.

Please get comfortable. Close your eyes if that helps you concentrate. When your mind wanders, gently pull your thoughts back to the words we're focusing on. Let's begin. Think about this verse:

"Be still, and know that I am God!"

Be silent for two minutes.

Then say, Think about this: "Be still, and know that I am."

Be silent for two minutes.

Say, Now, "Be still, and know."

Be silent for two minutes.

Say, Now, "Be still."

Be silent for two minutes.

Then say, Now, "Be."

Be silent for two minutes.

End the silence by saying amen. Ask these questions:

How did you respond to this exercise?

How did the silences feel—too long, too short, about right?

Did you feel like we were wasting time that could or should have been spent in conveying or gathering information?

Invite conversation in pairs for three minutes. If there is time, allow comments to the whole group.

LECTIO DIVINA (45 MINUTES)

This week's passage is Ephesians 2:12-15. After the time of reflection and prayer, invite group members to note in their book anything they want to remember from the time with scripture.

CLOSING AND PRAYER (5 MINUTES)

Ask participants to reflect on what singing or listening to the Lord's Prayer means and has meant to them, which musical version(s) they especially like, if any, and why.

Tell the group that you will be inviting people who choose to do so to speak a sentence prayer. Then, after all who wish to have prayed, you will end the prayer.

Take the bowl or container with the notes about prayer that the group members wrote at the beginning of the session. Pull out one piece of paper and read aloud what it says. Pass the container to the next person to do the same and continue around the circle.

When the container comes back to you, say a sentence prayer of your own to start the prayer. After all have spoken, close with this prayer or one of your own:

God of many names, God of all love, help us always to pay attention to our heart's yearning to know you. Continually deepen our conversation with you, that we may understand your will for us and live it more fully day by day. Amen.

NOTES

WEEK 1

1. Chaim Stern, ed., *Gates of Prayer for Shabbat and Weekdays: A Gender Sensitive Prayerbook* (New York: Central Conference of American Rabbis, 1994), 139.

2. Abraham Joshua Heschel, *Moral Grandeur and Spiritual Audacity* (New York: Farrar, Straus & Giroux, 1997), 258.

3. See Psalms 68:5; 89:26;103:13.

4. Dr. David L. Lieber, quoted in *Psalms of the Jewish Liturgy: A Guide to Their Beauty, Power, and Meaning* by Miriyam Glazer (New York: Aviv Press, 2009), 1.

5. The Most Rev. George Carey, Archbishop of Canterbury, in an address to the General Conference of The United Methodist Church, Cleveland, Ohio, May 10, 2000.

6. The Hebrew language uses consonants and "vowel points," not actual letters, to indicate where vowel sounds occur. Adding the vowel sounds of Adonai to the four letters Y-H-W-H creates the word *Jehovah*, which many speak of as representing God's name.

7. See http://www.jewfaq.org/name.htm for examples.

8. Chaim Stern, *Gates of Prayer: The New Union Prayerbook* (New York: Central Conference of American Rabbis, 1975), 135.

WEEK 2

1. Dr. Howard Olds. Unpublished sermon delivered at Brentwood United Methodist Church, Brentwood, TN, March 16, 2003.

2. Ibid.

3. Tom Gildemeister, sermon at Christ United Methodist Church, Franklin, TN, June 28, 2008.

WEEK 3

1. Karla Kincannon, *Creativity and Divine Surprise: Finding the Place of Your Resurrection* (Nashville, TN: Upper Room Books, 2005), 32.

WEEK 4

1. "A Service of Word and Table IV" in *The United Methodist Hymnal* (Nashville, TN: Abingdon, 1989), 26.

2. Karl Barth, from *Deliverance to the Captives* (New York: Harper & Row, 1961), quoted in *Weavings: A Journal of the Christian Spiritual Life*, X11, no. 6 (November/December 1997), 37.

3. Emmet Fox, *Sermon on the Mount* (San Francisco: Harper-Collins, 1966), 170.

4. Douglas V. Steere, *Dimensions of Prayer: Cultivating a Relationship with God*, rev. ed. (Nashville, TN: Upper Room Books, 2002), 45–46.

5. Numerous sources cite statistics regarding armed conflicts: the Ploughshares Project, the U.S. Institute for Peace, the Carnegie Endowment for International Peace, and various other nonprofits working on the links between hunger, poverty, and war.

WEEK 5

1. Mary Lou Redding, "Clean White Boxes," originally published in *alive now!* magazine, May–June 1982.

WEEK 6

1. Chaim Stern, *Gates of Prayer: The New Union Prayerbook* (New York: Central Conference of American Rabbis, 1975), 616.

2. Walter Wink, "Waging Spiritual Warfare with the Powers" in *Engaging the Powers* (Minneapolis, MN: Augsburg Fortress, 1992), reprinted in *The Weavings Reader* (Nashville, TN: Upper Room Books, 1995), 97, 99.

3. E. Glenn Hinson, "Not Giving Up," in *Weavings: A Journal of the Christian Spiritual Life*, XXII, no. 4 (July/August 2007), 12.

4. See Rubem Alves, *I Believe in the Resurrection of the Body*, trans. L. M. McCoy (Philadelphia: Fortress Press, 1986), 70.

5. Ibid.

LEADER'S GUIDE

1. Dietrich Bonhoeffer, *Life Together: The Classic Exploration of Christian Community*, trans. John W. Doberstein (San Francisco: HarperSanFrancisco, 1978), 82.

2. For more information on this way of reading scripture, see "Reading Scripture Devotionally" in *The Meeting God Bible* (Nashville, TN: Upper Room Books, 2009); Robert Mulholland, *Shaped by the Word: The Power of Scripture in Spiritual Formation*, rev. ed. (Nashville, TN: Upper Room Books, 2002). For leading groups in *lectio divina*, consult Norvene Vest, *Gathered in the Word* (Nashville, TN: Upper Room Books, 1997, o.p.).

3. This exercise is adapted from *Companions in Christ: A Small-Group Experience in Spiritual Formation*, Leader's Guide (Nashville, TN: Upper Room Books, 2001), 101.